"In *Embrace the Beat* ing bare—from messy et) to messy diapers, to barreling into the school drop-off lane with only minutes to spare (like the crazy-haired, pajama-clad mom-goddess you are) and then trying to feel sexy with your lover later—Stephanie takes each issue head-on with passion, empathy, and sometimes a charming and appropriate-for-the-moment foul mouth, which is incredibly endearing because you know that she knows what it's like when you just want to shut the effing bathroom door. Not only does Stephanie get it, she gets you—an overworked, overstressed, but overjoyed mom. Stephanie is more than a parenting coach, she's your BFF, confidante, and cheerleader in this amazing thing called momming (which really should be a real word by now). I'm giving this book to all my mama friends so that when they're on their last thread of sanity, they can open the book, breathe, and embrace this moment of beautiful chaos that, before they know it, will be gone."

"I laughed. I cried. I yelled 'This is so me!' in numerous places. I totally feel this book and am so grateful to have read it. My favorite parts are the sassy attitude, cursing, personality and the affirmations given to moms throughout the book."

—Lindsay Flanagan, Writer, Editor and Mom of 2

"I have read a lot of relationship books, but nothing that has been as relatable for me as Part 2 of this book. I started reading it today while at the gym. I was going through ALL OF THE EMOTIONS! The man next to me must have thought I was nuts. Seriously, one of the most relatable books I have ever read."

—Polly Foster, Graphic Designer turned Stay-at-home Mom of 4

"The writing is engaging and personal. It feels like you are sitting having a conversation with a close friend. It is approachable, accessible and authentic. Loved it!"

—Patti Monaco, Marketing Executive, Mom of 3 grown children

"After the first couple of chapters, I noticed I was waking up happier and with a more positive outlook on my day."

–Nathalia Capelini, Realtor and Mom of 3

"I could not put this book down. I loved the stories and examples throughout the book that were entertaining but still taught me something useful for my day to day life."

–Nora Pawar, Yoga Instructor and Stay-at-home Mom of 1

"This is the perfect book to read at the end of a long day to unwind. It's full of great reminders. It's extremely relatable - totally nailed it!"

–Adrienne Hamilton, Part-time Real Estate Agent and Mom of 3

"What an encouraging, candid, much-needed guidebook for moms. Stephanie brings her expertise in navigating chaos to help her readers stay centered and (somewhat) serene when things are falling apart around them. This is the book you need right now."

–Martha Bullen, Book Publishing & Marketing Consultant and Mom of 2 grown children

Embrace the
Beautiful
Chaos
of Motherhood

Embrace the Beautiful Chaos *of Motherhood*

The Secret to Staying True to Yourself

Stephanie Pereira

Better Together Press

Copyright © 2020 by Stephanie Pereira
All rights reserved. This book may not be reproduced, transmitted, or stored in
whole or in part by any means including graphic, electronic, or mechanical without
the express written consent of the publisher except in the case of brief quotations
embodied in critical articles and reviews.

For permissions or for information about special discounts available
for bulk purchases, sales promotions, fundraising,
and educational needs, contact:
http://www.embracethebeautifulchaos.com/contact/

For more information and to contact the author for speaking or coaching,
visit: http://www.embracethebeautifulchaos.com

ISBNs: 978-1-7348674-0-4 (print)
978-1-7348674-1-1 (ebook)
978-1-7348674-2-8 (audiobook)

Printed in the United States of America

I dedicate this book to my three incredible children,
who have helped make me into the woman I am today,
as well as my best friend and soulmate for doing this thing
called life with me. There will never be enough words to
express my love and gratitude to you guys.

Rebecca Ann –
Celebrating you♡ – your
life, journey + motherhood!
Here's to embracing the whirlwind
craziness with love, grace + joy!

Keep shining!
♡ Stephanie

Contents

Introduction   1

Part 1: Reconnecting with Yourself Amid the Chaos   7

     Chapter 1: Find Your Amazingness (Believe Me, It's There)   9

     Chapter 2: You Are Awesomely Amazing   19

     Chapter 3: Self-Love: You Can't Fill from an Empty Cup   27

     Chapter 4: Expectations = Unnecessary Stress   40

     Chapter 5: Perception and Thought Processes   47

     Chapter 6: Follow Your Joy, and Joy Will Follow You in All Areas   60

Part 2: Reconnecting with Your Significant Other Amid the Chaos   69

     Chapter 7: Significant Others   71

     Chapter 8: Talk to Me, Love   81

     Chapter 9: To-Do's, To-Be's, and Not-to-Be's   88

     Chapter 10: Appreciation Goes Both Ways   99

     Chapter 11: Love and Sex: Handle It Like a Goddess   112

Part 3: All the Jobs Moms Do   125

     Chapter 12: Careers In and Out of the Home and Everything in Between   127

     Chapter 13: More Than "Just" a Mom   149

Part 4: Troubleshooting: Help a Mama Out   163

Introduction

The whirlwind of life with kids is no joke. After our third child was born, my husband and I found ourselves in survival mode. I barely had the time and energy to do the mandatory and necessary, let alone think of my marriage or myself like my mother-in-law had so wisely advised years earlier when I was pregnant with our first child: "Once the baby is born, make sure to still take time just for yourselves." But we just couldn't seem to get ahead of our plans, schedules, to-dos. I was a hot mess, my husband was stressed to the max, and our marriage was on its last legs, although, ironically, we were closer than ever after going through major life changes like moves, career changes, and, oh, right—three kids. It was chaos.

I know very intimately what it's like to be lost in that chaos, often blind to the beauty of it. I had neglected my well-being for years. While I had heard the sage advice my mother-in-law told me, I didn't really know what that meant as a mom. I was convinced that I needed to find the right book or program that would magically whip my life into the one I yearned for, but I was never able to find it.

Fast-forward to the present day. My life is totally different from what I described above, but it's all for the better. Much of the daily action and chaos hasn't changed, but what *has* changed is me and my response to the inevitable chaos. I'm now a top priority on my to-do list, as is my marriage and my relationships with my kids. Through several years of consistent self-care, I have found the peace within that I was so desperately looking for.

I also have discovered the secret to finding that beauty amid the chaos and will teach you all of those steps in this book. I will share my best perspective-shifting tips and break them down for you so you can immediately apply them in your real life. What good is a self-help book that doesn't help you do that, am I right? I'm super excited to start this journey with you, and I'm totally rocking out to "Magic Carpet Ride" by Steppenwolf in honor of the wonderful adventure we're about to begin together.

But first, a case study: a day in the life of a mom in a hot mess. A typical day for me before discovering the secret to finding beauty amid the chaos *wasn't* pretty. I woke up several times a night with my baby, finally drifting off to sleep in time for my alarm to ring. I rolled out of bed to get the boys ready for school. I woke up at the last possible minute and wanted to get ready as they got ready, but they needed me too much. They bickered with one another and with me, and they moved slower than molasses in January, completely indifferent to the fact that we were on a tight schedule. I needed to get them out the door so they could go to school, and I could check it off of my list.

The lunches that I wanted to pack were nonexistent, so my kids had to buy lunch; morning snacks were packs of whatever we had in the pantry, like it or not, which also served as breakfast. I felt guilty about this later, but whatever. They were fed, right? I had to rifle through a basket of clean clothes to find socks or clean pants. I ended up rushing the boys out the door, dropping an occasional curse word if there was some unforeseeable hiccup, like frost on the windshield.

Seriously, there were days that it seemed like *everything* was against me. Luckily, the school was only a two-minute drive from our home if I Dukes-of-Hazzarded my way over the speed bumps. We pulled in with seconds to spare, and I continued to rush the kids: "You need to RUN! I love you, now go, go, go!"

Once I got back home, I walked in and no sooner sat down than my daughter woke up, and it would be time to go through her whole morning routine. I tried to be happy, but I was exhausted and secretly wished she would just go back to sleep so I could too. I just needed to

Introduction 3

catch my breath. The day was filled with changing diapers and outfits, feedings, chores, and errands. I felt like I never stopped. I was always pushing through to the next thing on the list. In the afternoon, when my daughter napped, I tried to get some work done. I didn't feel like I was financially contributing to our family, so I pushed myself to work on a business I had started with minuscule success to show for it.

The boys rumbled into the house after school, and I wanted to lose it since my daughter was still napping. *Please.God.No!Do.Not.Wake. Up.Your.Sister!!* I was running on pure fumes. I had nothing to give to anyone. I got the boys another pack of something from the pantry or a piece of fruit as they settled in to start their homework. My daughter woke up, conveniently when my hands were messy, and I let out a heavy sigh because I knew she would get upset that I couldn't get her as quickly as she wanted. By the time I got to her, she was crying, and it took several minutes for her to calm down. Meanwhile, I heard the boys wrestling in the kitchen. I wanted to cry right along with my daughter but held back the tears. I headed back downstairs, prepped her bottle, and helped the boys with their sight words, math problems, and reading.

One of the neighborhood kids knocked at the door and invited the boys to play outside, and I felt slightly embarrassed that the house was in shambles as he took a glance inside. It seemed weird because I spent a good part of the day cleaning, and I wondered if another family secretly lived here that I didn't know about. How else could this place have been such a freaking disaster?! When the boys burst out of the door to join their friends, I breathed a sigh of relief that it was just the baby and me again. I tried to play with her while sending work-related e-mails or catching up on some chores that just didn't stop needing to be done.

Within minutes of one another, my husband arrived home, tired from his long day, totally stressed from work, and the boys returned with as much energy as they had when they left. We all wanted dinner, but I hadn't even thought about it yet. They were all disappointed when I said I had no idea what to make for dinner, and furthermore, I would have to get the baby her dinner first before I could even think about ours. I felt the stress rise in my chest as I fed her, wracking my brain for what we could possibly have to eat. I was slightly annoyed at the whole thought of dinner and wished everyone would just fend for themselves. Once I imagined what a catastrophe that would be, I revoked that original thought.

While he waited, also thinking of dinner options, my husband sank into the couch and drifted off to sleep without realizing it. My daughter had finally finished, and I needed to find something safe for her to do while I made dinner. I whipped up something as quickly as I could—ravioli for the second time in a week and put it on the table with a side salad as I sarcastically thought, "Look at that; not all superheroes wear capes."

My family ate while I got up repeatedly from the table to comfort my daughter, who wanted to be held and to play. I ended up eating my not-warm ravioli after everyone else had left the table. My husband played with the kids while I went toe-to-toe with the mother-effing kitchen. I definitely wanted to cry when I saw the huge mess.

I ended up giving the disaster zone the middle finger, and I headed to the couch for the first time in a few days. I was done. I had zero energy left and was utterly defeated. I still had more of the day to tackle, but I needed to just chill on the sofa for a bit. My master plan was a colossal failure because I wasn't even able to relax. My daughter saw me and wanted me and only me. She lay with me as the boys held a slam-dunk contest on the indoor basketball net in the same room, with a lot of loud dribbling, cheering, and slamming into things. I looked around and saw the dishes glaring at me from the kitchen. It was the slap in the face that I didn't need.

Since I had made the mistake of laying my exhausted body and soul on the couch, I was basically incapacitated. I didn't think it was physically possible for me to get up and do what I had to do. My future self would be just as screwed as my present self at that moment. I was drowning in my life, an onslaught of overwhelm and failure. I knew what I wanted to do but just couldn't seem to get it all together. It was bath time (finally), and I had to get through this. I dragged myself upstairs and helped my husband bathe the kids. All hair and teeth were brushed, pajamas were on, stories were read, hugs and kisses were exchanged—and I made a mental note to buy the *Go the F*ck to Sleep* book after the umpteenth good night.

By some miracle, the kids finally succumbed to that magical land of dreams all moms wish for—the stars had aligned, and all of the kids were asleep. That was rare! Usually, it was me and my little party animal who liked to stay up drinking (milk) until 2 a.m. I felt relieved and slightly lighter. I was in the home stretch.

I started my shower—and I heard the baby screaming. Shit! I winced and opened the shower door as I tried to decipher it, but there was no cry. It was only in my head. Whew! After I finished my shower, I slipped into my pajamas and headed down the hall to check on the kids. I admired the peacefulness each of them exuded as they slept. I said a prayer for each one, kissed them each once more, and felt so thankful to have these wonderful humans in my life. I felt blessed to be their mom. But then a voice started in my head, reminding me of everything I should have done differently that day. These kids deserved better, I thought to myself. I left their rooms, feeling defeated, and carrying a ton of mom guilt.

I climbed into bed, totally spent. Then I felt extra bad because I could barely put a coherent sentence together to catch up with my husband. When he asked about my day, I said it was fine and left it at that. I wished I had more exciting things to share, but my day made pretty boring news, and I was too fried to put a creative spin on it. I didn't want to talk to anyone or to do anything. I checked the clock and calculated the estimated amount of sleep I would get before the baby would wake up for her middle-of-the-night feeding if I fell asleep right at that moment. I let out another heavy sigh, gave my husband a hug and kiss, and rolled over to get some much-needed sleep. But then I remembered the kitchen was still a disaster, and I would have to deal with that the next day. What I needed at that moment was more than just physical rest. I needed peace. But I didn't know how to get it at that moment.

My intention for you in the upcoming chapters is to feel understood in the most challenging areas of motherhood and for you to better understand yourself and how to find your peace amid your chaos. This

6 Reconnecting with Yourself Amid the Chaos

is your journey—your struggles, your growth, your book. I'm excited to share all of my best tips and strategies to lead you to *your* peace. I'm not saying you'll float through your days like some Zen master monk lady, but you will probably find tons of relief in these pages and easily find more peace and beauty in your life on the daily. Each chapter includes invaluable tools that I have used and continue to use regularly to help myself fully embrace the beautiful chaos of motherhood. They include tangible ways you can apply the new info and affirmations and questions for deeper reflection. There is a quick reference troubleshooting guide in part 4 of this book, which includes a variety of strategies to help a mama out. Part 3 highlights the demands on moms both in and out of the home. Part 2 focuses on your love relationship and how to keep that thriving in the beautiful chaos. And in part 1, we focus on the woman behind the role of mommy and get you reconnected with yourself so you can ultimately be a better everything—woman, wife, mom, human.

Ready to step into your amazingness?

PART 1

Reconnecting with Yourself Amid the Chaos

CHAPTER 1

Find Your Amazingness (Believe Me, It's There)

Motherhood is a marvelous journey that will bring out the absolute best in us and in our lives. Our children are the reason for much of our success and fulfillment. We never imagined how much we could love someone before that little bundle of joy was placed lovingly in our arms. Many of us have dreamed of this since we were little girls. Walk into any card aisle and read the cards about motherhood, and you will feel the love, inspiration, and good vibes of having the honor and privilege of being a mother. It's such a glorious position and is deemed as one of the world's most important.

But what the greeting cards won't ever tell you about is stress, the nonstop work, and seemingly endless days in the trenches of parenting when we are pushed past our limits. Our well-being often takes a back seat in this whirlwind of beautiful chaos, and we may not necessarily mind or even notice at first.

The more you intentionally focus on your personal growth and well-being as a woman, the better mom you can be. The secret isn't focusing on what's outside of you, but what's within. We aren't looking to control or change the chaos of parenting, but rather to find the peace to be able to see the beauty of it all.

Moms Do It All

You name it, moms do it! Have you ever taken a second during the course of your day to think about ALLLLL that you do? To allow yourself to stand back in amazement of all that you are able to fit into twenty-four hours successfully? If I asked you to make a list of all the stuff you wanted to get done but didn't get to, or things that you should be doing but just can't seem to accomplish in your day-to-day life, I bet you could rattle off dozens of things. As moms, we are hard on ourselves. We have habits of focusing on what's missing, what we aren't doing but should be doing, and how we're failing. On the flip side, though, have you ever thought about all that you are doing *right*? Have you given yourself credit where credit is due for the good things you *are* doing for your family? I'd like to invite you to make a list and then just marvel in your productivity!

Here are just some of the things moms engage in on the daily:

CEO of the household: Cue Beyoncé's "Run the World (Girls)" as you step into your awesomeness! We run this motha! MOMS!

Alarm clock: For yourself and children, although they like to have turns in this part as well.

Lost possession finder: Remember, it's only lost if Mom can't find it!!

Laundry specialist: Making sure everyone has clean clothes that match and aren't too wrinkly after the third time being forgotten in the dryer (#sorrynotsorry) and performing major stain removal is no small feat!

Personal chef: Is it just me or is someone ALWAYS hungry and needing a snack and/or meal?!

Planner: of meals, activities, schedules—lists and lists and lists ...

Housekeeper: The house won't clean itself! Believe me, I've waited to see it, and it really doesn't.

LET'S NOT FORGET . . .

Encourager

Playmate

Best friend

Shoulder to cry on

Voice of reason

Teacher

Cheerleader

Chauffeur

Hostage negotiator

Crisis management specialist

Chief justice

Hairstylist

Director of child development

Family therapist

Disciplinarian

Student

Toy repair expert

Finance manager

Potty trainer

Personal assistant to each family member

Wardrobe stylist

Personal shopper

Playdate coordinator

Storyteller

Special event planner

Travel agent

Bodyguard

Nurturer

Referee

Professional Organizer

Buffer/Censor

Delegator

Coach

Correctional officer

Crossing guard

Diplomat

Disc jockey

Homework advisor

Hygiene consultant

Inventory manager

Nurse

Peacekeeper

Creator

Recreation director

Waitress

Volunteer

And so on and so on and so on . . .

This "quick" list highlights typical mom stuff that may occur through the course of any day, but it doesn't mention the pregnancy, birth, and working or being a wife, friend, daughter, sister, and all the other parts of our lives. Put all of that together, and it's no wonder we feel worn down all of the time! Are you beginning to recognize glimpses of your amazingness?!

Moms—aka Future Shapers

We have the opportunity to shape the future through our children. We wear so many hats within this one role that we call motherhood. It can be easy to feel overwhelmed by all of these things. I mean, no pressure, right? Only the weight of the whole freaking world—it is a huuuuge responsibility. We feel that pressure when we think of it, but what about in the ho-hum, everyday moments? When we see this bigger picture of our influence, it can make the daily sacrifice less draining and tedious—once we get past the fact that the future of mankind may be hanging in the balance.

> **There's such a disconnect in seeing our child's bright future as a successful adult and in us clearing the dishes after dinner or reading a fairytale before bed, that often it's impossible to see the value of what we do as moms.**

It's never one specific task that a mom does for her child that makes the child great, but a collection of tasks and moments that accumulate over time that mold them into someone amazing. I wish we could have a better idea of how our "menial" tasks will influence our children as we are doing them, but the best we can do is to remember our upbringing. If we reflect on the examples of our parents, guardians, teachers, coaches, and friends, we can often begin to make the connection between their everyday actions and the lessons they taught us over time. Many of the world's greatest leaders and celebrities attribute their success to their mothers. Some of these fantastic people are Facebook COO Sheryl Sandberg, President Abraham Lincoln, Pablo Picasso, Maya Angelou, and Kevin Durant, among millions of others throughout history. You are one of those meaningful moms, making a difference through the life of your child.

Lost in the Chaos

I've been there, and that's why I'm here with you, right now, in these pages. This book is for the mom who is overextended, exhausted, and overwhelmed, who sinks into her day as she comes face-to-face with task after task for her to tackle. At one point, she thought she had her life together, but currently, nothing could seem further from the truth for her. Her mind never stops: she has lists and lists of things to manage, plan, and figure out; countless moments spent worrying about a myriad of concerns. She feels the weight of the world on her shoulders and has no idea how she will be able to do it all—or even part of it—well. She questions her abilities daily and tries her best to push through and keep doing what she has to do while sacrificing herself in the process.

I *was* that mom. I know what it's like to struggle, trying everything to keep my head above water, thinking I just needed more time, and then I would be able to get everything together. I was overwhelmed, and this stress was spilling over into the other areas of my life. I was at a breaking point. I knew something needed to change. I was tired of repeatedly hitting the wall.

A friend of mine told me of a therapist he was working with in Brazil and shared some of the benefits with me that he was experiencing. She wasn't a traditional therapist. He explained that she worked with energy and helped her clients release whatever was holding them back. Sounded simple enough. I was so desperate for relief from my anxiety, overwhelm, and chronic exhaustion that I was open to try just about anything. So, even though this path was very different from my traditional upbringing, I reached out and scheduled my first appointment and began my adventure of self-care and understanding. At the time, I didn't know that the solution was within me, like it is in Dorothy right when she lands in Oz. I was convinced that I just hadn't found the right book, program, teacher, or religion to get all of this craziness under control. I was looking for an outside source of help.

Yes, my therapist was terrific for me, but she always stressed to me that the healing wasn't coming from her. She was a facilitator of sorts for the healing that I was coresponsible for. She held the space for me until I could do that for myself, and I love her for that. The difference in my life from no self-care to ongoing self-care has been phenomenal. I have rediscovered a lot about myself and have found my "Zen" in spite of the continued craziness of my life.

My life events haven't changed very much as far as chaos levels are concerned. I still have three beautiful kids, and I'm still in the thick of parenting, but what once was a stress or hassle to bear is now lighter and easier. What has changed has been my *response* to that stressful hassle. I have the tools now to help me process the triggers and find my peace even when all hell is breaking loose around me. I'm calmer. I'm more loving. I'm a better person. I've let go of many past traumas and old beliefs that were the root cause of much of my frustrations and stress. Yes, there are times that I still get anxious and feel overwhelmed, but they don't consistently run my life or moods anymore.

And that's what I want to share with you—all of those tools and techniques that can help you find that better place mentally and emotionally. These are things I have learned in my life, and I want to share them with you. I can't promise your results will be the same as mine, but I *can* swear that I've been changed by using these tools. And if you think about it, you want results that are best for *you*, not my results. I've designed the chapters to be customizable so you can get yourself closer to *your* best results. All you need to start is a commitment to find your best you. Because she's in there. I'm going to show you how to make yourself a priority, because if you're not taken care of, pssshhhh, you sure as hell can't expect to take care of others.

> **How we take care of ourselves is, ironically, the foundation of being a fantastic mom.**

How Well Are You Embracing the Chaos of Motherhood?

Before we dive into the life-changing goodies waiting for you, it's important to get really honest with yourself and identify where you are in your beautiful chaos. This is the first step to applying the secret of finding your Zen: focusing on yourself and taking an honest look at your current situation. Don't worry about getting all judgy on yourself. If that comes up for you, that's OK, but try to put it aside for a sec while you answer with the first response that comes to mind.

IS YOUR CHAOS RUNNING AMUCK?
ANSWER THE FOLLOWING QUESTIONS TO FIND OUT.

1. Do I wake up exhausted even after a full night's rest?

2. Would I like to spend time on myself doing what I enjoy, but I rarely get the chance?

3. Am I more sarcastic or snappy with others than I would like to be on a regular basis?

4. When something goes wrong and I react to it, do I usually feel guilty afterward or wish I would have handled it differently and maybe even promise to do better next time?

4. Do I have a consistent habit of escaping from the overwhelm in ways I know I should be better about (bingeing on social media, TV, food, shopping, etc.)?

6. Do I feel like there's too much to do and never enough time to do it?

7. Do I have a hard time accepting help from others?

8. Do I feel overwhelmed by everything I have to take on as a mom?

9. Do I often say yes to things even when I really want to say no?

10. Have I forgotten what I was like and enjoyed doing prior to having kids?

If you answered yes to any of these questions, welcome to my world! You are understood here. If you answered yes to *all* of these questions, double welcome! I was in the exact same spot. We are overwhelmed, and life can feel frantic. Most days may feel like a blur, and we find ourselves on autopilot because the relentless onslaught can all be too much sometimes. All right, there we said it! We've established it. Now let's get the party started. Real relief is on the way!

CHAPTER 2

You Are Awesomely Amazing

I hope the laundry list of common mom tasks in the last chapter pumped you up and helped you begin to see how much you bang out every day and how incredible of a feat that is while still handling everything else you've got going on. I know some people have a hard time with that list and feel that it's such a heavy responsibility. Yeah, I totally agree that being a mom is an enormous amount of work. But what if instead we looked at it from a different angle and placed our attention on feeling honored to be a mom? I'm not talking about a guilt trip for ourselves of how lucky we are to have kids while many families struggle with that. What I'm talking about is simple—recognize the fact that to our kids, we are their whole world. We are the most important person in their lives for many years. No one else can fill that spot. EVER, NO MATTER WHAT. We are their go-to. When I get really deep in this thought, I can't help but get emotional. To know that I am so loved and so revered by my kids in spite of all of my flaws and shortcomings is almost unbelievable to me.

Noticing Your Amazingness

Realizing my amazingness wasn't easy for me at first. Of course, there were areas that I had an easier time with, but there were some areas in which I was not giving myself the credit I deserved, and I had a tough time changing that around. I remember one instance when I received a compliment from a friend on becoming fluent in Portuguese. She was

19

giving me props for learning another language and praised me for teaching it to my kids as well. I deflected the comment because "it took me several years to learn it, and I married someone who spoke Portuguese, so, you know, it's really not a big deal."

A by-product of the work I've put into myself has become my increased ability to notice my worth and happily accept those compliments when they come my way. I no longer look for reasons to downplay the praise but bask in the honor of that moment. I've also found that it's easier for me to express sincere compliments to others. So let's try out how comfortable you are hearing nice things about yourself, shall we? Say these next phrases aloud and take notice of how they make you feel:

* I am incredible.
* I am amazing.
* I am a badass.
* I am a wonderful mom.
* I am enough.
* I am strong.
* I am doing AMAZING things daily.

How did you feel reading these statements? Was it easy to accept them, or were there any that didn't go down so smoothly? No worries if there were some that you didn't relate to yet. It's actually totally normal to get disconnected from these feelings, especially as a busy mom.

If there were any that didn't feel right but are how you would *like* to feel, let me introduce an *extremely* valuable tool for you to experiment with to help you realize your awesome amazingness: affirmations.

Life-Changing Mommy Magic

We all have our beliefs and thoughts that we perceive to be true for ourselves. These beliefs are really just thoughts that we have thought over and over and over again until they become so ingrained in us, they become a belief that we hold. OK, so what? There is enormous power here because you CAN change your beliefs—slowly, and one thought at a time, but you can do it, and, over time, the new thought(s) will become your new belief. LIFE-CHANGING MOMMY MAGIC!! The first step in changing a belief is introducing a new thought—a thought that you consciously, repeatedly think until it becomes more believable and eventually a belief of your own.

For example, let's say you notice that you are not a very patient mom lately and have been short-tempered with your child, spouse, or even yourself. Maybe you're impatient with everyone you come into contact with. If you choose to allow yourself to repeat, "I'm so impatient; this is terrible," over and over, you will not become more patient, no matter what else you try to do. However, if you instead respond with an affirmation, you have the potential to turn everything around, especially if you're at the beginning of realizing your impatience. Instead of affirming what you don't want, flip it for what you do want. The affirmation you could use in this case could be, "I am patient," "I am open to being more patient," or even "It's OK to take a breath; I have time to be patient."

When you notice a negative thought, make a conscious effort to modify it with an affirmation. You could say, "I am patient with myself and others," and you might make this a ritual at the beginning of your day, possibly stopping during your day to remind yourself of it with your affirmation, and again before bed. You can say this to yourself or aloud. I find it to be way more effective for me when I speak it aloud, and also if I write it down.

The goal is to take baby steps to start feeling better and to modify our beliefs (repeat thoughts) that don't match up with what we want for our lives. I want to be a patient person—patient with my children, my spouse, others, and myself. I choose patience now. I choose to rewire my thoughts to make this possible for myself.

Affirmations can be an amazing tool to help us change our thoughts. They have had such a gigantic impact on me that I have designed customized affirmations for each of the topics in this book. You can find these gems at the end of each chapter. Please take what works for you, modifying as necessary. If it doesn't resonate with you, please don't use it. Affirmations are most powerful when they create an emotional response within us, like a "hell yes!" feeling when we say it. If you can say something and feel that, you are on the right track with your affirmations.

Center of the Family Universe

As mothers, like it or not, we need to be on our thought A game, because, after all, we are the center of our family's universe. Have you ever thought of yourself in this way before? Is there a more badass way to see your importance as a mom? With myself and my friends alike, I see this proven true time and time again. It's often the root of one of our biggest frustrations. Moms are the rock of the family. Moms are the ties that bind families together—the lifeblood, the special sauce. Not that everything is about us or revolves around us. No way—far from it. What I mean by this is that we, as moms, are the guiding force, the grand master, the reason things happen and/or don't happen, the be-all and end-all of our family.

Even when we have partners who are fantastic at the whole parenting thing, the emotional load of our family falls primarily on mom's shoulders. We can anticipate needs, moods, and feelings before they are even expressed. I believe that's how we are hardwired as women. We are tapped into our families, and being able to offer that support and security is crucial to the easier functioning of our family's life. If we aren't careful, that help can come at a very high cost: our well-being.

If you don't see this, think back to a time when you were too sick to function or so swamped at work with a pressing deadline that you had to give all of your attention to it. How did that day go for your family? Did everything run smoothly, without a hiccup? Was everything that usually gets done on a normal day executed when and how it usually is? Or did all hell break loose? Maybe all hell breaking loose is a bit much, and maybe the house and family put themselves on pause for you. OK, everyone survived, but it was true survival mode, and typical daily occurrences had to wait for a day when you were better.

I see this clearly in my life with any back-to-school night or evening meeting when I'm not home, and my family is left on their own. I treat these evenings as social experiments for my family and purposefully don't leave a to-do list or any specific instructions. This is progress for me, because there was a time when the mere thought of doing something like this would have me hyperventilating into a paper bag. However, now I grab my purse, give everyone a kiss and hug, and depart with a big peace out! Mama has left the building. What happens each and every time is that my family members wait for me. Their day is put on hold. They keep playing or doing fun things, but the must-do tasks that are standard routine in our house are placed on hold. Now, I'm not sure if it's a "the cat's away, the mice will play" scenario, or an "I'm going to wait for Mom because she is part of that routine" thing. I come back, and there are times they haven't even eaten dinner. Sometimes they had something super quick and easy. But consistently, not one person has done one part of the standard routine in my absence. The same happens if I'm traveling for work, or if I'm under the weather. Go figure.

Now, think of a day when you wake up healthy but just in a funk. You know, one of those days that you can't even stand to be with yourself. Did the dynamic of your family change in any way? Usually for me, everyone is having some type of varied meltdown within fifteen minutes of the start of my funk, and the whole day goes to shit unless I actively change my funk and help everyone else out of it too. So the frustrating part of this being-the-center-of-your-family's-universe thing is that bad days and sick days aren't an option, even though they happen.

One random Saturday, I woke up feeling like I had just stepped out of the Monica video "Don't Take It Personal" from 1995, where she is having an off day and just wanted to be by herself. I was like, "No offense; just leave me alone, guys. I love you all, but I'm not really feeling it (or anything, for that matter) today." I don't remember why I was feeling this way; just one of those days, I guess. Everyone else in my family was up and in great moods. The boys were happily playing, and my husband was working on a project nearby. Within ten minutes of me gracing them with my funkiness, the boys were fighting like cats and dogs, I was spazzing, and my husband was pissed that the calm morning had morphed into something from *Jerry Springer*. I was annoyed on so many levels, but mostly because I couldn't just be in a funk for half a freaking hour! Seriously, live your lives without me for thirty damn minutes! A few days later, I was discussing this with a dear friend, and she exclaimed, "Yesssss!! What is up with that?? The same thing happens with me!" We then swapped war stories of how we recovered, and we ended up feeling less alone in this crazy fact of mom life.

We can see this as a total mom curse: We can never have a bad day or a day to be sick, wah wah wahhhhhh! It's just so hard and demanding to be a mom! Why are these people so obsessed with me?? Wahhhhh!! OR we can see the incredible influence we have in our family unit and step into that power. The point isn't *not* to be the center of your family's universe anymore, but to embrace it with grace, peace, and a whole lotta deliberate attention on yourself.

It's OK to Adore Yourself and Take in All of Your Awesomeness

I want a family who feels my endless love and pride. I want a family who knows they are capable and courageous. I want to lead by my badass example of being good with myself before anything else and acknowledging all that I do for myself, for them, for us.

I'm amazed at those moments that I can feel the palpable love from my husband and kids. They think I am beyond amazing, an incredible woman. While this is extremely important, the MOST important person's opinion of me is me. My family can adore me, but if I don't adore myself and take in all of my awesomeness, it's as if what they feel almost doesn't even matter. I need to be my absolute best for myself and also for them.

Take a second to stop and marvel at the lives that you were entrusted with. What an intense thought! These little ones chose you to be their mom. This is so special and so important. They need someone who will not only love them as only a mom can but who will also help bring them into who they are and why they are here, inspiring them to be the best versions of themselves.

We are raising the movers, shakers, and world changers. We need to step up our game as parents so we can do our best by them. They are looking to us, so let's be good role models and lead by example of loving ourselves. It's OK to realize who we are and what we do and to notice our accomplishments. Let's keep going with it and take pride in all of that.

Bottom Line

You are a mother-effing badass full of unique qualities. You are wonderful and amazing. It's OK to realize all that you're doing right and to allow yourself to take joy in those things. Play around with some of the affirmations from earlier. If they still feel too intimidating, try adding "I am open to . . ." before the affirmation. So, if it's hard for you to say, "I am incredible" with that "hell yeah" feeling behind it right now, try saying, "I am open to being incredible," and see if that feels a little better. If you don't feel a difference right away, that's OK. Just stay with it. With your intentional focus on reworking these beliefs about yourself, you are laying the foundation of everything else to come in the following chapters. Give yourself permission to see yourself in a new way and realize how amazing you are.

OK, fine, but how do I apply this IRL?

* Make a list of your day-to-day tasks and bask in your amazingness! It's terribly easy to feel lost in these tasks, I know. But to start, if you list out each thing you do as a mom, you'll easily see how those "little" tasks add up to a miraculous feat.

* Make a list of qualities that you admire about yourself.

* What are some things that you have done this past week, month, or year that you are proud of?

Embrace the Magic of Affirmations

❋ I am a loving mother.

❋ I love my spouse and children.

❋ I choose to see motherhood as an honor and a joy.

❋ I choose my thoughts. I choose love.

❋ I'm impressed by my daily contributions to my family.

Make sure they resonate with you. Modify as necessary, so you can get a "hell yeah!"

CHAPTER 3

Self-Love: You Can't Fill from an Empty Cup

Now that we have established how freakin' amazing you are at being the center of your family's universe, we need to get into an area that is usually the first to get cut during the daily chaos of family life—you time! I know you're laughing out loud right now, thinking this must be some type of joke—if you're already stretched to the absolute maximum, how in the world will you be able to fit ONE MORE THING into your day?!

Please bear with me here. The secret sauce in your mothering is how well you are able to love and take care of . . . **yourself.** You cannot fill from an empty cup. When you aren't being replenished and building yourself up and filling your own cup, you don't have anything to draw on to give to others.

> **There is no limit to what our lovely family will take from us, but there is a limit on what we can give of ourselves when we aren't intentionally and consistently replenishing ourselves.**

Our giving nature as moms often puts us in a position of making things better for our loved ones; sometimes this means by making a situation "worse" for ourselves or by taking away from ourselves. Sacrifice and motherhood go hand in hand, but when it's excessive and we aren't refilling, we are left completely empty. Once we get to this point, it's hard to make a quick comeback. Our loved ones might not even notice, as they are so accustomed to that one-way street of sacrifice that it doesn't even dawn on them that we've had more than we can take, physically, emotionally, mentally.

You probably know what I'm talking about if you've ever put your child to bed after a full and active day together. You have done the positive parenting thing all day, you've played with them, you've talked with them, and even though you're grateful for those moments, you are tired. You want to do something for yourself, and as the clock strikes 9 p.m., something's gotta give! You're keeping your parenting together until the umpteenth ridiculous request, and you think, "Please just go the f*ck to sleep already!" That's the point of "I've given all I have to give today, and I'm done—I have NOTHING else left." That's an empty cup.

Your kids will only see sarcastic, negative actions and comments coming from you when you're in this place. Let's be honest: if we aren't careful, there are days we already wake up in this place of having nothing to give to our spouse or our kids. We feel depleted. Those are the days when you just feel mad and then get mad at yourself for feeling mad. You know the days when you get on your own nerves, right? Not a good place to be in. It's impossible to be the best version of yourself from this place.

Time Just for You

Moms are the busiest people on the planet! I understand the amount of stuff and lives we are responsible for running and how many things we have to remember and stay on top of, or else things will start falling apart. So, with all of that, how can I justify taking one extra minute that I don't currently have for myself?! This question runs the gamut from moms of newborns to moms of teens. In every single phase of motherhood, you are at full capacity. If you have one child or seven, you are at full capacity. Where is this extra time going to magically come from, especially when there is more you would like to do and feel like you should be doing for your family than you currently do now?

Ok mama, here it is. In order to make sure that you're taking care of yourself physically, emotionally, mentally, and spiritually, you need to carve out time during your day just for you. It is possible. It may require some creativity. It may require asking for help, and it will most certainly require changing some beliefs around. But don't worry—there's a step-by-step guide in this chapter to walk you through. Please consider this with an open mind and be open to a new idea or new way of seeing or doing something in your life. It has been said that doing the same thing repeatedly and expecting a different result is insanity, so let's get down to finding what's working for you and what can be changed a little to bring about new results and the relief that you are looking for.

Please understand that what works for your sister or friend or the other mom from the playgroup may be a complete disaster for you and vice versa. Read over the following questions and answer honestly for you. Put the "Well, I know I should respond with . . ." on the shelf and get real with your responses. These questions are designed to bring your attention to your baseline for the time you have or could potentially have for yourself. Be sure to answer for *you*. There are no incorrect answers, because you are the one who knows yourself, your family, and your lifestyle the best.

1. What do I do for myself on a daily basis?

I used to hate this question. I would scoff and think, "Do for myself? Umm, nothing! I'm a mom!" I remember being in a mommy-and-me yoga class, and we were toward the end of the class. I had just had my third child, and she was with me while the other two were at school. The instructor was discussing the importance of self-care for moms and asked us to share what we did for ourselves on a daily basis. I heard the other moms say how they took a spa day at least once a week or how they had someone come in and watch their child while they went to the gym. One mom mentioned having time in the morning with a good book and a cup of tea. But when it was my turn, I drew a blank. In spite of my panic, I was able to muster up that instead of doing the dishes after dinner, I would go and relax on the couch for a little.

30 Reconnecting with Yourself Amid the Chaos

What I left out was that it wasn't truly relaxing because I could see the huge pile of dishes waiting for me, and it was more an act of trying to escape and being at a point of sheer exhaustion, but for the yoga class, it served its purpose. The other moms' reactions were polite, but my answer was so different from the others' that the instructor took the opportunity to make it a teachable moment and shared how something simple like that also counts. When her daughter was a baby, the instructor's daily "me time" consisted of putting on lotion.

So, with the question above, don't stress it. Maybe your answer is amazingly decadent, and maybe it's nonexistent. Most importantly, it needs to be honest. Don't feel too bad either way, because it's just for you.

2. In an ideal situation when time and money aren't an issue, what is something I would like to do for myself? What do I feel really good doing? How often would I like to do these things? Make a list of at least ten things you enjoy doing.

This is a loaded question. Suspending reality for a second, humor me, and think about what would be amazing for you. My mind goes straight to getting a massage on the beach in Bali or eating croissants under the Eiffel Tower. Obviously, I love to dream big! But on a more realistic note, I also like getting facials, listening to audiobooks, and walking on pretty nature paths. There were times in my motherhood journey when what I really wanted most was a nice, long, uninterrupted shower. The things you want will vary from stage to stage. After my daughter was born and I was a mom of three, I forgot what I really enjoyed doing. In the years leading up to her birth, I had focused on my sons and barely on myself. I knew I loved going out dancing, but was the hip hop room at a club in Philly really still my scene? To a certain extent, I had to rediscover what I liked to do. If you're hard-pressed to find at least ten things you'd like to do, go online and search for some things you'd like to try out to see how fun they are for you. This list doesn't have to be things that you've ever done before.

3. What are some indicators when I have an empty cup? How do I feel? What do I do and say (my knee-jerk reactions)?

When the boys were little, I went to the dentist for a routine checkup with the kids in tow. I asked the hygienist why my jaw would pop or click when I tried to open it. She then asked me if I clenched my jaw often, to which I replied, "Of course not!" She raised an eyebrow, glanced at the boys and back at me, and said, "Honey, you have a three-year-old and a two-year-old and a popping jaw. I'm sure you clench it." No sooner did we get home than I noticed my first clench. I kind of froze for a sec and was like, "Would you look at that?! I am clenching. HA!" If several busy days go by, and I haven't had time for myself, I begin to feel anxious and can hold that anxiety in different places in my body, like my jaw or my shoulders. I get restless and feel like I need to just go, go, go and push through it all, too. I now know that when any of these indicators pop up for me, I need to take a deep breath and say, "Let's slow down a bit," and I focus on upping my time for myself and bringing it back as a top priority.

4. What could I do today or this week for myself?

Depending on how your list turned out of things that you enjoy doing or would like to try, this question will be easy. If you had more of a fantasy list like me with the trips to Bali and France, this is the time to think of practical things you like doing that are accessible for you on the daily. I can definitely sit and enjoy a cup of tea. I can listen to my favorite music. I can dance around the living room. I can call a friend to catch up or take a walk at a park nearby. I could schedule an overdue facial or haircut. The options are endless here. It doesn't have to involve an airplane or a lot of money. Some of the most fun things to do are free anyway. Make sure these are all things that make you feel good and bring you peace. Meditation is HUGE for me. I love using a variety of guided meditations to help me stay balanced and feel good. YouTube is full of great guided meditations for free, so all you need is an Internet connection and a few minutes. There are lots of apps for this as well. For a free guided meditation for relief from stress and overwhelm by me, please go to my website for your free download. www.embracethebeautifulchaos.com/resources

5. How do I feel about doing things for myself?

My answer to this one changes from time to time. I love to do things for myself because I have seen the dramatic improvement in my life from doing so consistently. There are times, though, that I still feel like I have a lot going on and just need to get stuff done. I am including this question so we can think about how receptive we are to the idea of taking time for ourselves. There was a time when I didn't think I had a right as a mom to think outside of that role. It wore me down quickly, and I needed to reevaluate that mindset. At the times I consistently pushed through and neglected time for myself, there was always a part of me or my life that would rebel and would force me, one way or another, to slow down and rest, like me getting sick or the kids being sick or something happening around the house.

Energy & Vibes

We all know the answers to your questions only matter if you can put them into practice, right? I also know how counterintuitive this process seems. I always thought that the more I had to do, the less time I had to slack off. I needed to buckle down and get to work—get it done, crank it out. I didn't think it was possible to slow down for things to work out better, but this was before I knew about energy. No, not the energy that comes from calories, but the energy that each person has—their vibration. Each person emits a vibration reflected by their emotions, which sometimes is very easy to notice when you get "vibes" from someone, good or bad. We've all seen that one guy who gives us the creeps—there you go, vibes!

So, when I take time for myself to get centered and balance my emotions, my energy is smoother, no matter how crazy my surroundings. Things go smoother for me. Events that I would have usually been stressing out about work out just fine, or even better than expected. I've started doing something pretty radical because of this that I have to share with you.

On my craziest days, I double down on my self-care or at least find ways to bring in more fun and enjoyment into that day in every possible way. I try to do this proactively if I know I have a tough day ahead. I fill up my cup ahead of time so I have more than enough for myself and others. I know it sounds illogical. I didn't even believe it until I noticed how well it was working for me. It wasn't something I had started doing intentionally for this result. I was just having fun learning about energy and meditation and stuff. I started spending daily time meditating before work with guided meditations. The results were stunning! I was calmer and made better decisions, and my time seemingly multiplied even though I was "taking time away from work to do this." This was one major piece of the Zen puzzle for me.

The only way you can see if this principle is true for you is to try it yourself. It's easy for us to rationalize that we don't have time for practices like meditation, exercise, or other self-care. This is like saying we don't have time to drink water because we're late for a marathon or put gas in our car because we're late for a road trip. How can I expect you to be able to do this? If you are at max capacity and you have a very, very busy day, how can you possibly dedicate extra time to yourself for any of this stuff?!

I don't think it's as much about what you are doing as it is about how you feel when you are doing it. Busy days can be draining and stressful. If we can incorporate things that are fun for ourselves and have a more enjoyable feeling, any day becomes better, especially a hectic one. It's also not about the quantity of time as much as it is about the intention behind it. When I mentioned that I double down on my self-care, I don't mean that I take a half-hour meditation and stretch it into one hour. I mean that I make it a nonnegotiable priority. Even if that means I need to do a ten-minute meditation in place of a half-hour one, it's a must do for that day because I need to protect my energy. If we take five to ten minutes to focus on meditation and be in those moments as fully as we possibly can, the effects will be felt throughout the remaining hours of our day. It doesn't even have to be sitting crisscross applesauce, eyes closed, with optional chanting. It can be as quick and simple as walking outside and noticing a beautiful sunset or a graceful bird soaring above and absorbing everything majestic in those moments. It can be sitting quietly in your car, taking several deep breaths. It can be getting a facial, massage, or haircut. It can be savoring a delicious meal. You're fully present and fully engaged in the enjoyment of the moment. You'll find a great amount of peace and restoration for your soul in these moments.

Time Is Whatever We Perceive It to Be

Let me introduce a cool concept that I've discovered on this journey of increasing time for myself on the particularly draining days. Drum roll, please ...

Time is an illusion. My guess would be that the Dalai Lama, Oprah, and that mom of multiple kids who is always put together, has the kids dressed well with their hair done nicely, and who arrives early to places all have this concept down pat. They probably know that they can expand their time as needed. They become the source of time and can do whatever they would like to do with it.

Basically, time is whatever we perceive it to be. Here we are again, back to our beliefs—so if we believe there are never enough hours in the day, we will be correct and always be rushing with a never-ending to-do list and feeling the pressure of always being behind. If we see time as something we can control depending on our perception and energy, we can shift into beliefs of always having enough time to do everything we need to do. We can be amazed at all that we are able to accomplish in a day. We have done this our whole lives without realizing it. Think of all the easy examples: "Time flies when you're having fun," "A watched pot never boils," etc.

This became clear to me when I first started working with my energy therapist. Prior to working with her, I was a frazzled mom of three, trying to keep up, but never able to accomplish half of anything. I was so frustrated with this, and it was one of the first things I discussed with her. "I feel completely overwhelmed!" I moaned to her. "There's never enough time to do anything that I need to do, let alone like to do. I never have time for myself, and I'm tired of all of this. I can't take it." She heard me out and then gave me the tools to change this story for my life. We worked together for a couple of weeks, and I began to see a difference.

My overwhelm was less. Instead of focusing on e
getting done, I was focusing on everything that w
the overwhelm creep up, I used this affirmation'
I can accomplish in a day." My morning didn't zip by ..
to be twenty minutes. I had time to complete tasks and even inu.
some time in there for myself. Changing this mindset indirectly took
care of the monstrous to-do list as well. I didn't see it as impossible. I
now saw it as everything having its own time, and everything would get
done in that time. The less I worried about it and the more I just did it,
it would work out with WAY less stress for me.

Change Your Thoughts, Change Your Life

You might be thinking, "Really, Stephanie? Are you telling me that if I
'change my thoughts on this,' my life will magically change? Come on,
my thoughts can't be that powerful!" My dear friend, yes, I am telling
you God's honest truth. Change your thoughts and change your life.
Remember that thoughts become beliefs that dictate our reality. You are
in charge of your life. You are in charge of your thoughts. It's better to
think things on purpose than to just let the thoughts come. A lot of us,
myself included, get caught up in the thoughts that keep coming and let
them carry us away. If we are more intentional with our thoughts and
take the time to think about what we want and how we want to feel, we
will notice our thoughts becoming real-life stuff.

Let's run through a scenario together. It's a Tuesday evening; you're
making dinner. Everyone has already expressed feeling hungry but is
excited about the tacos you're preparing. Your husband is away for the
week, and you're holding down the fort the best you can. Your adorable
four-year-old is prancing around the kitchen island, loudly singing the
same line from the *My Little Pony* theme song over and over. There are
two ways this could potentially go down:

necting with Yourself Amid the Chaos

on 1. Mom has a full cup

AND I DON'T MEAN A MARGARITA!)

You took time earlier in the day to do something for yourself. You feel balanced and, at this moment, you have an easier time feeling the joy of your daughter freely dancing and singing in the kitchen. It's easier for you to notice the beauty, the sparkle in her eyes as she peeks at you as she rounds the island for the thirty-fourth time. You not only see the magic of this moment but soak it up and cherish it. You know from your older kids that this phase flies by and soon will just be a memory.

Option 2. Mom's got an empty cup

Things have been crazy. You didn't have a chance to do anything that you wanted today. You still have so much to do and are feeling behind. You're more easily annoyed by the song and become resentful that you're cooking. You end up missing all of the goodness noted above. You might get pushed to the point of no return when you reprimand your daughter, saying something you don't really mean (that she may never know or believe that you don't mean). In your irritation, you might send a message to her that you don't like being around her if she is happy or enjoying herself, possibly guiding her indirectly to dull her beautiful sparkle.

I didn't intentionally make the second scenario as dramatic as possible, but I did want to point out the possible repercussions. Some of the things that have stuck with me the most are simple scenarios from my childhood when someone reacted and said something that indirectly affected me. No one intentionally said or did anything to dull my sparkle, but there were moments that led to that result. As an adult, I now understand that those comments were never about me. They were merely a reaction of someone who wasn't devoting time to themselves and who'd had a long, hard day and didn't have a lot of patience for the four-year-old in the room. The four-year-old me didn't always understand that, though.

Self-care has been a strong foundation for my days as a parent, and I'm so grateful I found it when I did. There were many days when I was operating from an empty cup. I know that I was doing the best I could with what I was working with at that time in my life, but I'm very thankful to be in a better place now, and it just keeps getting better.

The Best Gift for Your Family Is Your Best Self

You deserve to be on your to-do list. Your family is counting on you, and the only way to be your best for them is to take care of yourself physically, mentally, emotionally, and spiritually. It's OK to take some time from your day and focus on yourself. You will be a better mom for it. You will be a better wife for it. You will be a better person for it. Your job is too important to only do halfway. It's not enough to be there, merely going through the motions. You need to be there and really embrace yourself and your family in each moment. Commit to yourself a small portion of time each day to take care of your needs. It's not counterproductive. If you spend an hour each day, that's less than 5 percent of your day spent doing something for yourself. It can include anything that makes you feel good, from reading, dancing, or painting to pampering yourself—anything that you truly enjoy doing. You will get way more done from a place of feeling good and experiencing well-being than you ever could from having an empty cup.

OK, fine, but how do I apply this IRL?

In order to fully embrace the beautiful chaos of motherhood, we need to take care of ourselves. Our families will not only understand and make out OK, but they will be much better off when we are in a good place. You can be a better version of yourself when you are rested and taken care of. When you allow yourself to be a part of your daily routine, taking time to focus on yourself, you fill your cup. This will probably look a little different each day, and that's OK. Remember, it's not what you're doing that matters as much as the satisfaction it brings to you. Explore this idea of putting yourself back as a top priority and what it looks like for you by answering the following questions:

* What do I wish I had more time to do?
* What would I like to do for myself in the following areas?

> Physical
>
> Mental
>
> Emotional
>
> Educational
>
> Creative/Self-expressive
>
> Spiritual

* Was there a time that I was on my to-do list? What did I do? How did I feel? Do I miss that?

* How do I feel when I am not on my to-do list consistently?

Now is your time to commit to taking back that first priority place for yourself. Give yourself permission for self-care. Place your hand over your heart and recite this aloud as many times as necessary:

I, _____(your name), give myself permission to be number one on my to-do list and will make this time for myself: _____
__ (number days a week, hours a day, etc.), not only for me, but for everyone that I love and care for, so I can be a better version of myself for them.

Embrace the Magic of Affirmations

* I take care of myself so I can better take care of others.
* I am calm and peaceful. I welcome personal growth and open my heart to receive and give love.
* I love myself. I believe in myself. I support myself.
* I am amazed at all that I can accomplish in a day.
* Making time in my schedule for myself is helping me and everyone around me.

CHAPTER 4

Expectations = Unnecessary Stress

After reading the last chapter, you might feel unstoppable, and that's fantastic, but please don't do what I did! I'm a recovering perfectionist and need to warn you not to fall into the same trap that I did with the whole me time thing. Whatever I do, I try to do my absolute best. I like to dream big and to have things go as planned. A word of caution after falling flat on my face: don't get so caught up in the perfect execution of your me time that you sabotage yourself. Sound impossible? Well, for years, I had a goal of eating healthy. I would wake up, drink my water, have a healthy breakfast, and feel proud of myself. I would have a good lunch and feel proud of that—look at me meeting my goals! Then I would come home and eat a not-so-healthy snack, which would lead to a few more and a few more, and soon enough, my healthy habits were thrown out the window.

I'm not bringing this up to point out my lack of self-discipline but to illustrate that I was never able to say, "OK, so that didn't go as planned. Let me get right back to it and have a healthy dinner, grab some water, or choose any other healthier option." No! Instead, I would call it a wash and indulge at dinner and dessert and always opt for a sugary drink instead of water. My expectation was to have a perfectly healthy day of eating, and when that didn't happen, I was stressed and mad, and then I completely undid the good I had done earlier in the day. If this happened on a Thursday or Friday, I would write it off until Monday. Isn't that when you're supposed to start dieting-type things anyway? This was a

40

big way that I was sabotaging myself. My expectations were not realistic.

When I went to schedule my "me time," I had an unrealistic expectation of waking up an hour or more before everyone else in my family so I could meditate, journal, work on affirmations, and do some yoga. You may have heard of the seemingly zillions of people who do this already and rave about all of the success they've had as a result. I noticed so many people talking about this and was intrigued. I wanted to implement it into my life! One of the main points of this practice, which I completely understand and agree with, is that you should wake up early to dedicate an hour (or more) to yourself to ensure you're setting yourself up for a productive day. Logically, this makes total sense. It's important to note that anyone who knows me knows that I am a self-proclaimed night owl and am not fond of early mornings. To give you an idea of this, when I was in high school, I would sleep in my clothes so I could push back my wake-up time by ten minutes. Early mornings and I weren't a good mix. Needless to say, my early morning me time lasted for four short days. It wasn't due to a lack of desire, discipline, or trying. It was because I was miserable.

Adjust Your Methods, Not Your Goals

While self-care is one of the best things I can do for myself, getting up an hour early was NOT the best option for me. I was rigid with my rules because of my expectation to have my me time in the morning. On day five, after a night of being up multiple times with one of the kids, my alarm sounded and I grunted, "Ugh, already?!" A big "hell no" resounded in my brain, followed by the immense pressure and guilt from not following through and the prediction that my day would be horrible if I didn't force myself past the exhaustion and make it work. I had this idea in my head that it was the "only possible time" I had, and it had to be that or bust. Well, it busted. I was frustrated and annoyed with myself and the early mornings, but later that day, I realized that I had about an hour of unscheduled quiet time. The kids were all at school, and I had finished up a project I was working on earlier than expected. If I wanted to, it would be the perfect time to do my self-care, but I wasn't happy about it. I was angry. I didn't want to do it in the afternoon because it didn't match my expectations. I was convinced that it would be impossible to get the same result if it were any other time of the day. After all, the zillions of people who swore by this method weren't doing it in the afternoon!

I caught myself in this ridiculous thought and questioned my expectations. Why did it need to be in the early morning? Was the predawn "self-care" worth all of the stress and frustration it was bringing? I needed a time that would work for me. I thought that I had it all figured out, but I kind of didn't. I didn't want to admit that to myself, but once I did, I was able to enjoy that spontaneous hour and felt great for doing so. I also learned that afternoon me time is highly effective!

Please, please, please take my lesson as your own and be flexible in your methods and only stubborn about your goals. Now, my me time varies from day to day, but I make an effort to have it every single day because that's what works for me. Now that the stress is removed from requiring it to be a certain time and way, I'm more spontaneous, and it's more enjoyable for me. Be sure to identify what *you'd* like to do while being flexible in *how* it's done. Don't get trapped in a cycle of self-sabotage, thinking things need to be a certain way to be right. And I don't know about you, but what works in my house one day may not work the next.

> **Flexibility with the "how" is key!**

It's all about a constant assessment of my thoughts, goals, and expectations. Are they a match? Is what I want the most coming to me in the easiest way possible? If so, I pat myself on the back and keep doing what I'm doing. If not, I need to reevaluate by stepping back and taking a look at the big picture. I need to be clear on what I want for that area and open to new ways of getting me there.

Unrealistic Expectations Lead to Some Pretty Icky Stuff

I would notice similar things happening in other situations, too. If I had expected something to go in a way that it didn't, I would feel frustrated, irritated, and automatically stressed. We all know these feelings don't bring out the prettiest side of us moms. True story: I was at my son's soccer practice that ran over by half an hour. My plan for dinner was to make this new recipe find from Pinterest. I made sure we had all the necessary ingredients, and I was on my mom A game that day. I even mentioned to the family how excited I was to try this new recipe earlier in the week. When we finally got home forty-five minutes later than expected, and dinner wasn't ready or even started, I was ticked off. I made the "WTF face" and threw my hands up in the air.

Writing it out like this, I can see how silly this sounds, but in my defense, I have a history of becoming irrational when hungry (don't we all?!). This is the main reason I carry snacks with me wherever I go. My purse is usually stocked, and sometimes I'll even share with the kids! But getting back to the point, on that particular day, I was irrationally angry with the situation, my husband, and myself! How in the world was my husband supposed to know that I was thinking of making that one dish for dinner, and since soccer ran late (which I hadn't even texted him about), he should have made it? It's nuts for me to expect him to read my mind in any situation. I mean, of course, there are times that he does, and it's incredible! He's an amazing man who I'm usually on the same page with. There have been many similar situations when I've come home and dinner has been ready. The problem with this whole scenario was my EXPECTATION. I *expected* something from my husband that I didn't communicate. I was a little irritated with him, but more so with myself. Being hangry didn't help, but the bottom line was that my expectation was completely unrealistic, which resulted in unnecessary stress for my family and me.

The good part of situations like this is that I'm now reminded to check myself. From this experience and other irritations over the years, I've gotten into the practice of questioning my expectations—all of them. I often question expectations of myself, my spouse, my kids, daily situations, and so on. Are my expectations realistic? There is immense power in assessing your expectations. There is always such a push, especially for women, to do things perfectly. Well, sister, be prepared to think for yourself. Be prepared to be honest. What do you expect from yourself? Your spouse? Your kids? Your day? This phase of your life?

A saving grace for the example above is that I was able to go easy on myself. I didn't spend too much time beating myself up. When the schedule didn't go as planned, I was understanding. I didn't get my panties in a bunch. I let my schedule change and kept moving on. When someone reacted differently from what I expected, I did my best to see their perspective from a place of love and just rolled with it. It's crucial to be gentle with yourself always, especially when things don't work out as we would have liked. It's necessary to be forgiving of others as well when they don't live up to our expectations. It doesn't matter if something works or not. It's in the process of trying where the real learning and growth takes place. So, you tried a new routine or tried to incorporate me time into your schedule and it didn't work? It might have even been an outright disaster—that's OK. No need to scratch the whole goal. You can always try again. You can try over and over and over.

One of my favorite affirmations to use during moments like this is, "Things are always working out for me." I have repeatedly seen that even when things don't necessarily appear to be working out for me, they really are, even if, in the moment, I don't understand how.

We Can't Control Others

The same way that we can't always control situations the way we would like, we certainly cannot control others, regardless of how hard we try. This even holds true for our kids. It's no secret that people expect parents to be able to control their children. We've all been there, dodging the glaring, disapproving looks from total strangers while our toddler temper tantrums down the store aisle. There are whole websites dedicated to showcasing reasons for toddlers' tantrums ("I want red cup! Not blue cup!"), but somehow we are supposed to be able to control our kids and get them to stop crying on demand. Depending on the day, it might be easy to influence our children, especially at a young age, but we can never, ever completely control them. We can teach them. We can love them. We can set good examples. We can make suggestions and discuss things, but ultimately the other person will only do what they choose to do. We can only control ourselves and our thoughts.

I remember the first time I realized this as a parent. It was terrifying. My oldest was a year and a half old at the time, and I just remember thinking, "Oh shit! This is not what I imagined! Now what am I supposed to do?" Before having kids, I thought I would be an excellent parent. I watched *Super Nanny*, and I was even a teacher. Having kids proved to me that I knew *nothing* about parenting. I knew I loved them more than life itself. I knew that I wanted to get better every single day at being the best possible mom for them.

Of course, we adapt and get very creative with ways of enticing kids to do what they should, but ultimately, they are in control of their actions. The best example is trying to get a child to apologize when he or she doesn't want to. You can talk to him until you are blue in the face, but he will only give that heartfelt apology, *sincerely* apologize, when he feels it. *He* decides. *He* is in control of his actions.

With this in mind, consider the expectations you have for your children. Are they too big? Too small? Too specific? Is there a way you could modify your expectations of each of your family members (yourself included) to a more realistic place for this phase of your lives? Re-assessing these expectations is the best way to eliminate unnecessary stress in your life. Of course, there are expectations we set that will be just out of reach for our children, and we hold them to that to help them grow, supporting them all the way. That's us doing our jobs as parents. In examining your expectations of yourself, your family members, and every other important area of your life, you will determine what a healthy expectation is, which is one that promotes growth and what a stress-producing, energy-sucking expectation is, which should be changed to something more positive or completely removed.

OK, fine, but how do I apply this IRL?

If we choose to be flexible with the "how" of our expectations being met and are open to questioning our expectations when they aren't being met, we're in a better place to embrace our beautiful chaos. Motherhood is full of high-demanding moments that will test our level of flexibility daily. The better we can adapt and keep the bigger picture in mind, the easier time we will have in accepting and handling these situations that are typically totally out of our control. It's guaranteed that oftentimes things will not go the way we plan, but our response to that is where our power is. We don't have to lose our cool and flip out. We can choose differently. We can choose to breathe and readjust. We've got this.

Ask yourself the following for more insight on your expectations:

* What expectations do I have of myself?
* Are these expectations realistic for this phase of my life?
* How can I modify them to better suit this phase of my life?
* Are there any expectations that I can mute for now or for good?
* Are there any expectations I would like to add?
* What are things I can do or say to myself when I start to feel upset, irritated, or angry when my expectations aren't being met?
* How do I feel about the idea of not being able to control others?
* Is there a time in my life that I learned this the hard way?

Embrace the Magic of Affirmations

* I can choose my thoughts.
* I can never get it wrong because I can always course correct.
* Nothing I do has to be perfect.
* Everything is always working out for me one way or another.
* I choose to see my _____ (spouse, child, myself, etc.) through a lens of love.
* I can always make a different choice now and at any point of today.

CHAPTER 5

Perception and Thought Processes

We've all been in that situation when we have some type of beef with someone. The reason doesn't matter for this example, but we know how it goes. There was a disagreement of sorts, our feelings were hurt, and we're annoyed and/or angry with this person. When this annoyance is active within us, we will perceive every word and action by this person as an attack. It's through our perceptions that we take in and process every experience in our lives. Our perceptions are our glasses that dictate how we see our world. They're always based on our beliefs. We may be aware of these beliefs, or they may be so ingrained in us that we don't recognize them as our belief but more of "that's just the way it is." Is the person who we have the beef with really a bad person? Or are we influenced by our irritation with them at that moment? Of course, we see them through the lens of irritation, which changes the whole perspective for us.

Imagine waking up on a sunny spring morning with the birds singing. You can hear them from your bedroom. Which "lens" you're looking through will determine how you respond to that moment. Let's say you woke up happy and are in a good mood. You're looking through a happy lens and, in noticing the birds' song, you become even happier. After all, you love spring, and it's such a wonderful way to start the day. Your next-door neighbor might have a different disposition that morning and choose to see the same situation through a grumpy lens. Your neighbor

47

will curse the noisy birds and possibly even the sun for shining so bright. Same situation, but very different reactions based on each person's perception.

There is a natural flow of our perceptions and how they play out in our lives. A perception always, always, always starts with a belief that we have. Sometimes we're aware of these beliefs and choose them deliberately, and other times they're buried deep in our subconscious.

> **Those beliefs create our perceptions of everything that goes on around us.**

These perceptions are then materialized through our thoughts. The thoughts are transformed into words, behaviors, or actions. Sometimes actions become automatic and turn into habits. Our habits dictate our values, which ultimately determine who we become.

Beliefs (conscious and subconscious) ▶ ▶ ▶
Perception (filter) ▶ ▶ ▶ Thoughts ▶ ▶ ▶ Words ▶ ▶ ▶
Behavior/Actions ▶ ▶ ▶ Habits ▶ ▶ ▶ Values ▶ ▶ ▶
Who We Become

The very basis of this, where *EVERYTHING* begins, is in our beliefs. I'm not referring to a religion here—I'm talking about what we believe to be true about ourselves: the "I Am" statements that we accept about ourselves and our lives. There are two sides to this, the positive and the negative. We have positive beliefs about ourselves that will naturally bring in prosperity and success. However, we all have some negative beliefs as well. These beliefs can be seen playing out in our lives too. They're the root of the limitations we place on ourselves. They don't feel good. They are heavy and burdensome.

Are there any areas of your life where you feel stuck? There is most likely an associated limiting belief "keeping" you there. The good news is that you get to CHOOSE what you believe. Remember that a belief is just a thought that you've repeatedly thought with conviction?

So the best news of today is that YOU CAN CHANGE ANY AND EVERY BELIEF THAT YOU NO LONGER NEED. Even better news? Your emotions will help you navigate through this process on both sides. If there is a good-feeling belief, that is a sure indicator that this particular belief is helping you. On the other hand, if there is a belief that doesn't feel good when you think it, but instead is heavy and disappointing, that is a sure indicator that the belief needs to be modified.

All Beliefs Are Changeable If We Believe They Are

Beliefs don't just come out of nowhere. Many of our beliefs come to us by default. We've either picked up others' beliefs as our own or have observed our pasts and made our own stories based on those. In the following examples, I present some common limiting beliefs for moms. In the next section, we will break down each belief to understand how change is possible. In order to change these beliefs, it's necessary to first recognize them. The first step is becoming aware of what the belief is and how it feels. You can't understand or change what you don't see. A prerequisite for all of this is to believe that this desired change is possible. Otherwise, you don't stand a chance, sweetie.

How to Change Your Beliefs

There are five steps in the process of changing a belief. These steps will work best for beliefs that you no longer need or that are preventing your growth. There are many beliefs you have that are helping you and, while they can always be amplified, the focus of this exercise is on those pesky, limiting beliefs.

The five steps are as follows:

Step 1. Recognize the statement/belief.

Step 2. Ask yourself how this feels.

Step 3. Understand what those feelings are showing you.

Step 4. Create your new belief.

Step 5. Take an inventory of your feelings and new beliefs.

Say whaaaat? It's OK. Let's take a look at three examples of different beliefs that we may or may not have as moms, and then let's change them.

BELIEF #1: *Things are always going wrong for me, even when I work to make them go right. I try to be positive and hope for the best, but something always goes wrong. Nothing ever goes my way. Even when things seem like they'll work out, I can't enjoy it because I'm worried that they'll take a turn for the worse.*

Step 1. Recognize the statement/belief. *Nothing ever goes my way.* Don't worry about judging or correcting yourself. Just simply notice this statement and begin to observe it.

Step 2. Ask yourself how this feels.
You may feel any combination of overwhelm, sadness, disappointment, anger, frustration, and fear. In the same way you noticed the belief, notice these feelings associated with it. Do you feel this somewhere in your body? Does your stomach drop, or does your chest tighten? The more you take note of your emotions, the more your ability to notice them will be like a muscle when exercised—stronger and easier to use.

Step 3. Understand what these feelings are showing you.
It's easy to skim over this step. It may seem obvious at first glance, but it can provide a deeper insight when we dig a little. Ask yourself, "What is this showing me?" You might take a look at only the surface. "It's showing me that I'm frustrated. Period." But dig deeper. Ask yourself more pro-

Perception and Thought Processes 51

found questions and really analyze this feeling. "Why do I feel so much frustration about this? What is this frustration trying to tell me? How can I shift this perception? How can I change this thought/belief? What would make this a little better?" Frustration comes when what we are expecting and what we are living don't match. In this example, it's an indicator that things are not how you want them to be. You want things to always work out. You want things to go right. You want to have a better life. The belief that you cannot have this better life causes frustration.

So go a little deeper—where did this belief come from? The answer will be personal to each of you. It could be the message you received growing up. Maybe your parents' lives were this way, and you unknowingly inherited their belief system. Maybe you had some experiences that led you to this belief, causing you to embrace it. Regardless of how it came to be, you can ALWAYS choose a new belief.

Step 4. Create your new belief.
You tend to get a better idea of what you really want by knowing what you *don't* want. As a result of you questioning your negative emotions, you have come to new information about your previous belief: *Nothing works out for me.* It's time to create a new belief that lines up with what you want. Sometimes it's as easy as believing the opposite: *Things are always working out for me.* But sometimes, it needs to be a little more subtle. It's not about just saying and repeatedly thinking, "Things are always working out for me." It's not about the words; it's about your feelings and your conviction. Is saying "Things are always working out for me" believable to you? Whatever you say with conviction and expect to happen is exactly what *will* happen.

Go easy on yourself and start gradually modifying your previous belief to something that feels a little better. It might be, "Things work out for me sometimes," or "I like when things work out for me." If you're saying/ thinking/believing these modified beliefs, you will begin to notice that more things begin to work out for you. You went from nothing working out and feeling complete frustration to sometimes things working out. That feels lighter. There is more hope in there. It feels brighter, and you will see this difference in your life as well.

52 Reconnecting with Yourself Amid the Chaos

Step 5. Take an inventory of your feelings and new beliefs.

This will be an ongoing process. Check in with yourself daily to see how things are feeling. Do you feel better about this area? Do you like what you're seeing in this area? Do you need to modify any of the beliefs? What would feel better? The amazing part of our lives is the constant growth and expansion. Each moment we have an opportunity to improve, to be a better version of ourselves than we were before. I love thinking of this process as a spiral instead of a line. That way, when stuff comes up that I've worked on before and "should be past," I don't have to feel defeated. It's just that at this point in time, I'm prepared to go deeper and grow more than I was the first time around with this issue. In every area, we can look for continued growth.

Fun, right? Let's do another one!

BELIEF #2: *Since having kids, my mornings have become very hectic and stressful. It's impossible to get everyone up and out of the door without some big drama. I always manage to get something spilled on my clothes, and I either have to change or look like a hot mess all day. We always end up late to school and work because it's such a disaster.*

Step 1. Recognize the statement/belief. *My mornings are an impossible disaster full of stress since I've had kids.*

Don't analyze it any deeper, just notice this belief. No need to try and make it better; just observe it.

Step 2. Ask yourself how this feels.

You may feel any combination of stress, failure, overwhelm, sadness, disappointment, irritation, frustration, and fear of not being a good mom. The same way you observed the belief in Step #1, notice these feelings associated with it here. Do you feel this somewhere in your body? Does your eyelid twitch, or do your shoulders tense up? The more you take note of your emotions, the more your ability to notice them will be stronger and easier to use.

Step 3. Understand what these feelings are showing you.

Remember, the deeper you go in this step, the more benefits you will see. Ask yourself, "What is this showing me?" You might take a superficial look. "It's showing me that I'm frustrated. Period." But dig deeper. Ask yourself more profound questions and really analyze this feeling. Remember the questions I posed above in Step 3: "Why do I feel so much frustration about this? What is this frustration trying to tell me? How can I shift this perception? How can I change this thought/belief? What would make this a little better?" In this example, you want your mornings to be smoother, with less stress and mayhem. You want more peaceful mornings. You want a better start to the day. The belief that you can't have this better life causes frustration. So go a little deeper—where did this belief come from? This answer will be personal to each of you. Regardless of how it came to be, remember, you can ALWAYS choose a new belief.

Step 4. Create your new belief.

Like already mentioned, you tend to get a better idea of what you really want by knowing what you *don't* want. As a result of you questioning your negative emotions, you have come to new information about your previous belief: *My mornings are impossible disasters*. It's time to create a new belief that lines up with what you want.

Since this belief is pretty extreme with lots of negative emotions linked to it, using the direct opposite, *My mornings are glorious and peaceful*, is not believable whatsoever. Remember, it's not about just saying and repeatedly thinking the new belief. It's not about the words; it's about your feelings and your conviction. It has to be believable to you. Whatever you say with conviction and expect to happen is exactly what *will* happen. This isn't something you can fake 'til you make it, because the power is in your feeling. If you're saying, "My mornings are smooth," without the same feeling behind it, you might as well say, "My mornings are a total disaster," because you will get the same results—guaranteed.

In this example, there is a pretty big gap between the current belief and what we would like it to be, so you can try modifying your previous belief to something that feels a little better. It might be, *My mornings are starting to run smoother*, or *I like when the morning goes smoothly*. If you're saying/thinking/believing these modified beliefs, you will begin to notice that your mornings begin to run a little smoother. You'll go from the morning being a total disaster and you feeling complete defeat to things starting to run a little easier. That will feel lighter. There will be more hope in you, and that is a good thing. You want to be able to feel some relief with your new belief.

Step 5. Take an inventory of your feelings and new beliefs.
This will be an ongoing process. Check in with yourself daily to see how things are feeling. This might be during your morning routine or shortly after. Reflect on the issue that was giving you trouble. Do you feel better about this area? Do you like what you're seeing in this area? Do you need to modify any of the beliefs? What would help you feel better? It's a good idea to question things until you get to a place where you're feeling better.

Our final example, Belief #3, is a pretty positive one compared to the previous two. There are minor improvements that could be made, but this belief feels much better, as it is open to possibilities. It's based on the fact that things have a way of working out and will continue to do so.

BELIEF #3: *I don't always know what I'm doing as a mom, but I usually follow my instincts and best judgment, and things work out one way or another. I know I don't have to have it all figured out to be a good mom.*

For this belief or something similar, you probably don't have much stress around it, and you wouldn't need to take this one through the five-step process. It's a good idea to recognize a belief and see if it's bringing peace or stress. If it brings peace, let it continue bringing peace.

It's a Process
At the beginning of this process, it's OK to see a lot of momentum in the opposite direction. You didn't create these limiting beliefs overnight, so it probably won't completely shift overnight either. It's a process. The power,

YOUR power, is in the present moment with the choice you are making right now. What are you choosing to believe now and going forward? That's where your power is. As Queen Elsa says, "The past is in the past!" It's one step that's repeatedly taken over time that completes a journey. As you become aware of what beliefs are working and which ones you are changing, you will also begin to create a positive momentum. Better feelings will pick up and begin to be more natural. Please be gentle with yourself during this process. It takes work and conscious effort.

A Note on Negative Emotions

Negative emotions are not "bad and to be avoided at all costs." When they come up, it's OK to feel them and explore them fully. They will ALWAYS lead you to what you need to know if you will take a deeper look. They are not to be suppressed and pushed down. That is merely a temporary fix that will come back over and over and over again until this issue is worked through, oftentimes on an ever-increasing scale, until you have no choice but to face it head-on. Allow yourself to feel your emotions, whatever they may be. Sit with them without judging or ana-lyzing yourself. Give a name to them and then release them. You might say something like, "I feel a lot of frustration. I wish this were easier, but I choose to let go of this frustration to make room for ease." Try your best to allow these emotions to come up and be released as quickly as possible. Feel the feeling, but don't become the emotion. Observe it, allow it, and release it.

A Note on Beliefs

No pressure here, but your beliefs are kind of a big deal. Be sure to create beliefs specific to what you want to see and materialize in your life and then focus on having them. There is a difference between saying/believing "I don't want to get sick" and "I want to stay healthy." I know I said that words don't matter, and they really don't, but try to feel the difference between "not getting sick" and "staying healthy." What matters most is how your focused thought or belief makes you *feel.* Can you feel powerful and healthy when you think "I don't want to get sick"? Umm . . . I can't. It makes me feel like there's a chance I *could* get sick, whether I'm aware of it or not. I feel worry and fear about that possibility, which is exactly what I *don't* want, since my goal is health. Saying "I want to stay healthy" is an easier starting point for health— it's closer to my goal. You can also think of it this way: the Universe will only say "yes" to you. If you are saying "I don't want to get sick," the focus of that thought is sickness. You don't want the sickness, but it's still the focus. Saying "I want to stay healthy" is the opposite since it is only focused on health. The Universe will say yes, no matter what.

> **"When you change the way you look at things, the things you look at change." Dr. Wayne Dyer**

The Power of Perception

In 2019, I heard an incredible statistic on the *Coop & Casey* radio show (on Philly's 96.5 TDY) that highlights the power of perception. It said, "Sixty-two percent of Philadelphians say the number one reason why they don't go to the gym is because they are too out of shape to go." Yes, you read that correctly! More than half of the people surveyed believe that they are too out of shape to go to the place where they could improve their health and fitness.

Aren't gyms designed for people to get into shape? Don't gyms offer programs and classes and personal trainers to meet you **wherever** you happen to be physically and work with you toward your fitness goals? Does this seem weird to anyone else? Each of the people surveyed had a choice to view themselves as being "too out of shape to go to the gym," resulting in little to no positive change. Alternatively, they could have changed their perception of the situation and realized that the gym is *exactly* where they can work on their fitness goals.

The survey didn't ask how many of the 62 percent wanted to be

Perception and Thought Processes 57

in better shape, but I imagine that most of them would like to be. As parents, we want to be healthy and able to keep up with our children. We want to be in shape. When we feel good about ourselves and our bodies, it's easier to feel good about everything else. A shift in perception is simple but not always easy. We always have to choose what we think and believe. Luckily for us, these beliefs, whatever they are, are never written in stone and can be edited as needed.

What we perceive to be problems and shortcomings in situations and people can always be reworked. These views can be changed into ones that feel better to us, and, when that happens, we notice the changes. We can choose to see others with love and view any situation through a lens of love. When you notice yourself getting caught up in a thought about your kids or husband doing something annoying *again*, take a breath and rethink it. Choose to see the person or situation through love. Of course, it makes total sense in black and white on this page! We love our families and our lives and should see through the lens of love always, but in our day-to-day lives, we don't always have that lens handy.

I get it. It's easy for me to understand this concept when I'm by myself, snuggled up with my inspirational quotes on Pinterest and sipping my chai tea, but ask me if it's just as easy once my kids are home, and I'm simultaneously making dinner, helping with homework (which involves concepts I have no recollection of ever learning when I was in school), and handling a preschooler's meltdown over getting the orange straw instead of the pink one. In these moments of utter chaos, it's my biggest opportunity to not only see through love but to be an example to my family of love in action. I don't always get it right, but when I do, I know that it's priceless and will carry on to my grandkids and beyond. I feel the power of a "mundane" moment and know that the ripples will go further than I can begin to imagine.

The momentum you start when you begin to change your beliefs (as we discussed earlier) applies in a similar way here. If I'm getting into the habit of looking for the good in people and situations, appreciating them, and making the choice to focus on the positives, it will be MASSIVELY easier for me to find the good and positives in

58 Reconnecting with Yourself Amid the Chaos

the next moment with them. The momentum will make it easier and better every time. The opposite is equally true. If I'm in the habit of pointing out what I don't like (even if I'm disguising it as "constructive criticism") and focusing on the negative, it will be easier for me to find what I don't like and what's wrong. Appreciation will be nonexistent. My outer life will reflect whichever side I choose to focus on most. Most commonly, we tend to have a bit of momentum on each side, depending on the person and situation before us. You can actively change that, though. Awareness of what you are focusing on (positive or negative) is the best first step. You always, always, always have the choice of what you give your focus to. Are you looking for the good or finding the bad out of habit?

I can usually tell when I need to change a limiting belief, because it's something I don't want to do. I mean, there is a lot of resistance on my part even thinking about it. I know there is an area causing me stress, and I've been working on myself long enough to know when something needs some attention by the wonky feelings coming up in relation to it, but in those moments, taking a deeper look is the last. freaking.thing.I.want.to.do. I dig my heels in sometimes and stay stuck in the stress much longer than I need to. What I'm asking you to do isn't what you will necessarily want to do at that moment, but darling, if you push through that hesitation to look at your beliefs on a deeper level, you will open yourself to a new, more enjoyable life for yourself and your family. I promise it is all worth it!

OK, fine, but how do I apply this IRL?

Isn't it cool to know that we are in charge of our beliefs?! There was a time in my life when I just thought my "reality" was absolute reality and that I didn't have much say in it. I didn't understand the influence my beliefs and perceptions had on it. There were some beliefs I was able to change as easily as flicking on a light switch and others that I wasn't. Some were very deep rooted, and I was only able to change them with time and support, and some only with energy healing. The important takeaway here is that change IS always possible if we are open to it. Take a look at the following questions and suggestions to start working on some of your beliefs that you would like to change for the better.

* Is there a belief you have that is holding you back from what you want? If so, what is it?

* If it's hard to identify one, think of a stressful area in your day-to-day life. Do you believe that area has to be difficult? Do you believe you are capable of figuring it out? Do you believe you can handle it?

* Once you have your belief that you would like to rework, ask how you feel about it. What feelings come up for you? Are you angry? Doubtful? Anxious? Frustrated?

* What is underneath these feelings for you? What's the deeper issue?

* What would you like to believe instead?

* What would feel better? What feels possible for you in this situation? What would be your dream come true? Write out your new belief!

* How do you feel? Better than before?

Embrace the Magic of Affirmations

* I can choose my beliefs.
* I can choose change.
* I choose to see this situation with love.
* I feel good when I rewrite my old beliefs.
* New ways of thinking can be magical.

CHAPTER 6

Follow Your Joy, and Joy Will Follow You in All Areas

This might sound crazy, but life is meant to be enjoyed and FUN!! As adults, we can get swept away with our responsibilities and the less enjoyable parts of life. It's easy to take ourselves too seriously and cut ourselves off from potential fun that's waiting in just about any moment. It doesn't have to be this way, you know. We get to decide how we live our lives, right? We are finally grown-ups, after all. We've waited our whole lives for this time, and here we are, but are we really living the dream?

Whatever You Focus On Grows

Think of someone you know who, in your opinion, has a seemingly fun life. This is the person who is usually in a good mood, has a great sense of humor, takes trips and adventures, and always has amazing stories to tell. This is the person who absolutely lights up any room they're in because they are radiating JOY and a zest for life. Do you know someone like this?

OK, now that you're thinking of this awesome person, take a second to observe their life as best as you can. Would you say they are operating from a place of abundance in their lives most of the time? Are they healthy? Are they in a loving relationship? Do they have a great group of friends? Do they have a decent financial situation? On a scale of one to ten, how satisfied would you guess they are with their life?

The people who come to mind for me are healthy and usually open for an adventure. They all have wonderful relationships with family and friends. They are endearing. They have enough financially to do what they'd like to. I would guess they would all rate their satisfaction with their lives at 8.5 or higher. Of course, they all have hard experiences—an ill relative, stress with work, occasional conflicts with others, loss of someone important, personal issues.

> But something each and every one of these fun people has is a strong mindset with helpful beliefs that they actively nurture, and they consistently live an intentional life. They know what's most important to them and design their days accordingly. They live life with purpose. They're happy with life, not because of all that they have, but because of who they are.

OK, now think of someone else you know who isn't as chipper and upbeat. This is the person who is expecting average or below in any given situation and will openly express disappointment or irritation when things go that route. This is someone who doesn't have much energy to do things. They don't get excited too often and aren't that fun to be around. They shut out fun and many wonderful aspects of life. Do you know someone like this?

Let's consider those same questions to observe their life as best we can. The people who come to my mind that meet this description are usually not operating from a place of abundance in many areas of their lives. They have deep-rooted, limiting beliefs that are keeping them stuck. They either get sick frequently or might even have an ongoing condition. They have loving relationships but experience more strain and strife than positive people you know. They may or may not have a great support system of friends. They most likely have lots of beliefs that limit their finances, like believing they aren't worthy of having more than enough, or that because they didn't get a four-year degree, they are destined to live paycheck to paycheck. I would guess that people in this category would rate themselves at five or lower for life satisfaction. They don't usually have a strong mindset and let life happen to them by default.

> **They aren't happy with life, not because of all they don't have, but because of who they haven't become yet, which is also why they don't have what others do.**

Did your answers vary between the two people? My guess is that you had different answers for most, if not all, of the questions. If you were surprised to see the differences, extend your observations to other people you know on both sides of the equation. The more you observe, the more you will probably come to the realization that happier people tend to have happier lives.

So aren't they just happy because they have so much going for them? I mean, if I had_____ (fill in the blank) like so and so, I would be happier too. Well, I know it's easy to think that way, but that's not exactly how it works. If you're happy, satisfied, content, optimistic, etc., you're more likely to be open to opportunities that will further your good-feeling emotion. If you're depressed, sad, frustrated, mad, upset, doubtful, etc., you will be hard pressed to find yourself as open to recognizing opportunities that will improve your feelings and your situation. Whatever we focus on grows.

Identify Our True Sources of Joy

When you're not feeling so good, you can begin to focus on changing and then ease your way up the emotional scale to better-feeling emotions. You can rewire your beliefs. Two movies highlight this point well: *Yes Man* with Jim Carrey and *Bad Moms*. If you haven't seen these yet, I highly recommend them. Both films start out with the main characters in a funk. Things range from OK to terrible in their lives and don't show much promise of getting better. As the protagonists shift their focuses and mindsets, their lives begin to change for the better. They begin to experience more joy, more freedom, and more exciting and fulfilling lives. Both films end with the main characters in a completely different (and much better) place than when the films began.

Yes Man begins with Jim Carrey's character, Carl, saying no to everything fun in his life. He is in the funkiest of funks until he runs into an old buddy who is in town for a "Yes!" seminar and invites him along. Intrigued by their conversation, Carl goes to the seminar and accepts the assignment of only saying "yes" to anything and everything presented to him. As Carl opens up to new opportunities, his life becomes more enjoyable and transforms into the life of his dreams.

Bad Moms is about Amy Mitchell (Mila Kunis) and her life as a mom of two who has been consumed by the beautiful chaos of motherhood. She is unknowingly pinched off from her well-being until she has had enough. Once fed up with living life according to others' expectations, she decides to take it back and redefine what she wants her motherhood to look like. Her life and the life of her family transform during the film into one that is happier and more enjoyable.

Like these characters, we can also be honest with ourselves in identifying the true sources of joy and fun in our lives. We can then determine the things that aren't fun and that bring no joy to our lives, finding ways to do more of what brings us joy and to less of what doesn't. We need to be ruthless in our choices here. Our happiness is not only essential for our personal well-being but for our family's health. We want to be wonderful examples to our children. We can do no wrong if we are firm in this step, protecting our happiness at all costs. You know that list of things you would love to do? Do them! They don't all have to be done today, but take a step toward at least one of the things. You need to nurture your fun and your life. Life is designed to be enjoyed!!

I had an incredible real-life example of this as I chaperoned my son's field trip last year. We were on our way back from the aquarium on a major highway just outside of Philadelphia, and, as per usual, there was some stop-and-go traffic. The kids were great and, in true kid fashion, didn't let the annoying traffic dampen their fun. They were talking and singing and enjoying the moment. They also did something that we've all done as kids, which is to signal with arm motions to the tractor trailer drivers to blow their horns. The first truck driver we saw wasn't letting the traffic interfere with his fun, either, and the kids cheered as he honored their eager pleas and honked. The bus erupted in victory! Kids were hugging and giving high fives in celebration. It brought a smile to all of the adults' faces because that true joy is contagious. The traffic switched a little, and the driver was able to move ahead of the bus. The kids were sad to see him go but hopeful when the second tractor trailer pulled up next to the bus.

The kids were extra energized by the previous victory and approached this driver with even bigger gestures and more enthusiasm. This driver wasn't impressed. He had a scowl on his face and didn't blow the horn. The kids were disappointed, to say the least, and labeled this second driver as a "sour apple." They knew that it was his attitude and lack of being open to fun that prevented him from pulling the horn. The kids changed their chant from "blow that horn" to "sour apple" for a few moments until traffic shifted again, and we were back in line with the first driver who, once again, answered the children's request to blow his horn.

In this moment, I began to think of my own life and identify times that I was the fun driver and other times when I was the sour apple. This turned into something that was very meaningful and had a significant impact on me. How many times do we choose to be the second driver because we have deadlines to meet and things to do or when we just aren't in a very playful mood? How many times do I limit the fun I can have with my kids and in my life because of that endless list of stuff to do? Much like the traffic on I-76, the list will always be there—it's a given. Do I choose to be joyful and have fun in spite of that? Or do I let it affect my attitude and approach to life that is happening now?

Commit to More Joy

This topic of fun and how you enjoy yourself is an individual one and will vary from person to person. There is no right or wrong answer. There are people who thoroughly enjoy organizing and decorating their homes. It's a release for them, and they are in their element when they're doing this. It's not my thing. I feel overwhelmed when I even think about something like this. That's OK. What's right for one person may or may not be the same for someone else.

Bubble baths are a perfect example. I have friends who slip into an automatic state of relaxation just imagining a bubble bath—with a nice glass of wine, some candles, aromatherapy, the works. I know other people who see nothing remotely relaxing and enjoyable about that. No biggie! You know what you like and what's fun for you. You know what you feel good doing and what doesn't feel so good.

Take a minute and make a list of the things you enjoy doing. You can create three columns on the paper. In the first column, list things you enjoy or think you might enjoy doing alone. In the second column, list things you enjoy or think you might enjoy doing with another person (spouse, kids, friends, family, etc.). In the third column, list things you do that you do NOT enjoy doing. Once you have completed your lists, compare them. How much of your time is from the "enjoyment" side, and how much is from the third column? I know there are things we have to do each day that might not be our favorites (i.e., packing lunch boxes and putting away laundry). The intention of this activity is to bring awareness to the amount of enjoyment and fun you may or may not have in your life. Make a commitment to include more fun in your life, and give yourself permission to enjoy more. I'm not saying you need to start gleefully skipping around your house as you do the chores, but this added joy might be something more subtle, like listening to your favorite music or talking to a friend while you chip away at your tasks. You know yourself the best. Find what is enjoyable for you and ways to incorporate those things into your everyday life more.

The Better It Gets

You'll notice an upswing when you allow yourself to add more fun and joy into your life. Your attitude on life will shift, and new opportunities will open to you. It will get better and, believe me, the better it gets, the better it gets! Remember what I said about momentum? Having the momentum of fun and enjoyment is the best kind to have! Imagine the difference this will make in your family's day-to-day life!

Try to ask yourself in every situation what will make things more fun for you. What can you do to make this more enjoyable for yourself and others?

OK, fine, but how do I apply this IRL?

Looks good on paper, right? But how in the world are you supposed to apply this to *your* life? Well, it helps when you know what you like. With some practice, you can become very creative in making even the most mundane tasks more enjoyable for yourself, especially with all of the technology available today. Sometimes just setting the intention of having more fun during your day is enough. You will be more open to seeing the fun in each moment. Please understand, I'm not saying that every moment of your life should be high-energy, smiley bliss and that to have that kind of life, all you need to do is say, "I want my life to be high-energy, smiley bliss." No, no, no. You will still have boring moments. You will have shitty days or shitty sections of a day. It's just how it goes. However, those lackluster moments help you to appreciate the good ones on a deeper level. But it is realistic to pose the question to yourself, "What would make this moment better for me? More enjoyable for me?" You can further explore this by listing things you like to do. What is fun for you? When you're stressed, what's your go-to pick-me-up? If you aren't sure or are trying to cut back on your normal go-to's, like smoking, eating, or shopping, try these suggestions and see what you think:

* Put on some music! I love turning on a streaming service and letting the music find me. I select the genre that I am feeling and let the Universe work her magic for me.

* Dance to said music, but only if you like to dance. Pants and/or bras are totally optional (well, if you're at home, anyway).

* Think of a really funny movie you watched and loved, and search for the funniest scenes on YouTube.

* Change the air! If you're home, go out for a walk, even if you aren't outdoorsy.

* Light a candle and admire it. New smells and sights in a room have a way of changing things.

* Allow yourself to be silly! This could mean talking in funny voices or whipping your hair around for a few seconds like you're back in 1996 in the mosh pit with your friends.

* Speaking of friends, text or call one of your besties who helps you feel better.

* Whatever is fun and feels good, try and bring it into the moments of life that aren't so fun for you.

Embrace the Magic of Affirmations

* I can choose my thoughts today.
* I can choose to feel good.
* I choose to let joy guide me.
* I welcome joy.
* I welcome fun.
* The better it gets, the better it gets.

PART 2

Reconnecting with Your Significant Other Amid the Chaos

CHAPTER 7

Significant Others

The first six chapters were all related to us, our inner worlds, and making ourselves a priority. We've built a fundamental foundation for the next area that is so near and dear to our hearts, an area that, at times, can seemingly either make or break our peace as women. This is an extremely BIG topic for us moms: our husbands. This chapter can still be beneficial if you have a significant other, boyfriend, fiancé, partner, etc. I will mostly refer to this role as husband, but please substitute whichever appropriate title is necessary for your situation. Throughout this chapter, we'll talk about how to realize the most common stressors and how to best handle them as they pertain to our marriages/love relationships.

Aren't husbands just great?! They're terrific partners, lovers, and best friends. They have seen us at our worst and love us in spite of it. Sure, sometimes they can be stressful, the same way that we can be stressful for them. Marriage can be one of the most fulfilling relationships of our lives; yet, at its worst, one of the most draining. I'm sure we've all "been there and done that" at one point or another, maybe more times than we'd like to admit. Did you know that a 2013 survey conducted by *Today* of approximately 7,000 mothers showed that the average mother rates her stress level as 8.5 out of 10? Nearly half of those reported that their partners are causing more stress than their children. Our husbands are who we've signed up to do this thing called life with, yet they are often one of our biggest stressors! Our goal in this chapter is to drop a lot of truth bombs that will help us discover our answers regarding who is stressing who out.

I encourage you to question your beliefs, your expectations, and your goals—all of them, especially regarding your husbands. Some would say husbands are our biggest stressor, but I would argue that it's not our husbands at all. We lose a good deal of our power by giving them the ability to stress us out. So instead of thinking of *husbands* as our biggest stressor, we need to determine the true causes of the stress. In the next few chapters, we'll look at nine major stressors that can affect our marriages and how to fix them.

Perceptions and Partners

I'm certain that the first and foremost **biggest stressor is our perceptions of our husbands.** Let's be honest. Our perceptions of any given situation in our marriages may not be the most accurate nor the best, especially when it comes to a situation that makes us feel wronged. However, we will almost always feel as though our views are crystal clear and 100 percent accurate. Once we get our defenses up, it's hard to analyze any situation objectively.

For example, I'm sure we have all had something similar to this happen:

> An overworked and overtired mom someplace in the world hisses under her breath, "I mean, seriously?! He slept in for the umpteenth Saturday in a row and is now napping at 1:30 p.m.?? You've gotta be kidding! What about *my* nap? What about the fact that I was up with the kids since the ungodly hour of 5:45 a.m., and, as a result, the kids and I are in a funk?! I mean, he *alwaaayssss* does this! Who does he think he is? And what does he think I am?? That is some nerve! Ugh, I can't even!"

Whoa, whoa, whoa. Before we get too caught up in this example . . . let's take a deep breath and a big step back. In this example, the loving husband has slept in on yet another Saturday while the mom is up before dawn with the kiddos (P.S. For the sake of this example, this mom despises early mornings, OK?). He then proceeds to fall asleep again for an afternoon nap while she is reenacting a WWE throw-down sesh between The Rock and The Undertaker to (please, dear God, and all things holy), get the kids down for their nap so she can finally get a breather that she's needed since Tuesday. It's obvious that she feels wronged by her husband and sees his sleeping and checking out as a total slap in the face. She's irritated and feels unacknowledged. She might even be jealous that her husband gets to do exactly what she would like to be doing, as she woke up earlier, and sleep is a hot commodity as a parent. A nap is way more appealing than dealing with a whiny toddler. No offense to all of the whiny toddlers out there.

When the wife chooses this perception, though, she's choosing way more than just that. But Stephanie, you may say, that's the reality of the situation! Her husband is sleeping when he should be helping. I hear you. I used to think that way until I learned something that blew my mind. Ready for it?

> **Our husbands have perceptions of the same situation, and they differ in varying degrees from the one that we have!**

Let's go back to this example, only this time, let's hear the husband's perception.

An overworked and overtired dad reflects, "I love the weekends. My wife is the best! She gets up with the kids when they wake up, and they have a special time together. I'm so glad I got to sleep in. I was thinking of getting up with the kids, but she must've already been up and was so thoughtful not to make a lot of noise. This week was nuts! I needed the rest. I really admire the way she talks with the kids and how she always knows what to do and say. They really admire her too. I wish I had the same bond with them, but that must be a mom thing. I wonder what we can do today as a family. I know the kids need a nap before we can head out someplace, so I'll just wait here, and maybe my

74 Reconnecting with Your Signicant Other Amid the Chaos

wife will come and hang out with me once she gets them down for their naps. It would be cool if we watched a movie together and maybe even made out some while they nap, like old times. It's not easy to put them down, but she's the best at it. She's such a great mom." *Dozes off without realizing it after a very long and stressful week at work.*

Wait, what? His perception shows he will most likely be surprised when his wife doesn't come to watch a movie once she finally gets the kids down or if she is nasty to him later in the day. Neither husband or wife is a mind reader. If she acts out of resentment or frustration, he will be hurt and will likely further the cycle.

Remember: the power of our focus at any given moment will bring us our next thought, which starts the spiral. We get to pick if it's in an upward direction or not. What way do we want to go? Which wave do we choose to ride? In this example, it's OK for the wife to feel whatever comes up for her. She can analyze her perception and ask herself why she feels this way. She can identify how she would like to feel instead and start with that outcome in mind, and then she can think of things that could change to get her closer to that desired outcome. As a proactive partner, she should ask herself what she thinks her partner's perception is about the situation, and she should ask him to confirm if it really is as she thinks or if there's something else there.

The more open dialogue they have, the better the husband and wife get to know one another, and the less guesswork will eventually be involved, leading to less frustration, misunderstanding, and resentment. Imagine the wife's relief to hear her husband's perception and to share with him that she feels she doesn't know what she's doing half the time and that she needs more help. He thinks she has it all under control and allows her to shine in her role that comes so seemingly natural to her. But she feels differently. She needs his support.

If this mom has been doing her inner work and consciously reaching for better-feeling thoughts, she will be in a better position to see this situation with love instead of irritation. She will have already laid the groundwork for a smoother way out of her frustration. She will be more in tune with what her emotions are bringing up. It won't consume her and spill over into the next hours or even days. This wife will be able to acknowledge it and move past it, voicing her needs and thoughts openly and constructively to her spouse. They will be able to come up with a solution together instead of going to war against one another. She knows that the best foundation a marriage can be built on is appreciation and love, and she's willing to look at both perceptions of the situation to get to some common ground.

A lot of times, these triggers aren't the root of our problem, but only an indicator of a deeper issue. The wife isn't annoyed about her husband sleeping in just because it's about sleep. The deeper issue is that she feels all alone in the craziness. If her husband doesn't want to wake up, by default, she has to. She feels trapped, like she doesn't have a say, and resents her husband for having the choice.

I saw this in my own life when it came to bath time for our sons. There were lots of times my husband would whisk them off to clean them up while singing and playing. The kids loved it, and so did I. There were times, though, that I was super stressed, and so was he. I would ask him to take the kids for a bath, to which he would respond, "Nah, I can't today." I get that, people. I know those days that you just "can't." You don't have more to give. You have a lot going on, and you just aren't your usual awesome self. But what about the mom who is on the receiving end of the "nope, can't do it," knowing that it really doesn't matter because the kids are filthy and need to bathe no matter how anyone feels about it?

When this happened to me, I felt sad, rejected, less important than my husband. But what I took some time to realize is that in these moments, I was receiving info about unhealed parts of myself. My reaction always came from my unresolved issues with myself as a mom. I didn't know this for a while, so I didn't always take a deeper look. It wasn't about that moment, but what that moment was showing me about myself. Why would this make me feel so sad and rejected? Why did I feel less than? At the time, I had a lot of beliefs that needed to be reworked. In doing the work that we covered in chapter 5, I was able to identify the beliefs that I had about myself that needed some shifting and healing.

Another more recent example from my life is that my husband would tend to take a bite of whatever anyone was eating. No biggie, right? Usually it doesn't bother me, but there were a few weeks when it was becoming annoying. The irritation was building and building. There was a time that I reacted out of that irritation, snapping at him. "Seriously, what the hell? Get your own!" And no sooner did these words come out of my mouth than I started the internal dialogue of asking myself what was really bothering me. Why was this so annoying to me? What was the lesson? What needed work?

Through further exploration, I realized that I didn't have a chance to take my walks in nature while meditating or listening to music due to an abnormal schedule and having work being done in our home. I wasn't really doing that much for myself at the time, either. I was in reactive mode and was starting to run on fumes. So while I did calmly talk to my husband at a later time about taking bites from every person, every single time, and getting his input on it (he didn't even realize he was doing it), I also took from this situation the lesson of how important self-care is in motherhood or for anyone who has contact with other people. I also realized how quickly my batteries could drain and needed to be recharged. My beef wasn't with the bites of food themselves—well, except for that decadent lychee ice cream—but with sharing one more piece of myself. Since I wasn't filling my cup, I didn't have a lot to give, and the bites reflected this and set off this trigger. If I didn't investigate my irritation, it could have been chalked up to my hungry hubby annoying me, leaving it as his issue when it was really mine on a deeper level.

Out of Control

A second stressor is that we think we are or need to be in control. If you have been or are in a situation like this with your spouse, you've probably wished you could just make him do something or be a different way, right? It would be much easier that way instead of dealing with all of this reflecting and self-analyzing. You probably start to feel increasingly frustrated when you are unable to make him do or be whatever it was that you thought was best. And it's not that you're crazy and wanting your needs over his, it's that you're thinking what would be best for *him*. Sigh. Even the best, most in-love couples go through their rough patches of marriage. If you aren't experiencing this now, you probably have at some point.

Not being able to control a situation with my husband is something that used to consistently push me over the freakin' edge! I was talking about this just a couple of chapters ago. Honestly, it still gets me every once in a while. "How can he not get it? It's not that hard! Just do what I'm saying, and it will be easier. Who does he think I am? Why doesn't he trust me? WTF!!" Well, with sixteen years of a happy marriage and counting, I have learned something that has CHANGED EVERYTHING!! Brace yourselves for another incoming truth bomb:

I cannot EVER, EVER, NO MATTER WHAT, control my husband.

I can explain my perception and my opinion and give my advice, but the final decision of what he does or doesn't do is COMPLETELY, 100 percent up to him. He gets to decide how he feels and will react in any given moment. I can try to convince him of something until I'm blue in the face, but it will only work if that's something *he* chooses to do. He's the only one solely responsible for himself. The same is true for me. I'm solely responsible for myself. There isn't anything my husband can make me be or do without my agreement. The final decision of how I act, think, or feel comes from me and me alone. So, when I finally learned this, I'm talking *finally* got it, my life changed. My marriage changed.

I wasn't as stressed, especially about my husband. There was so much pointless drama over me wanting to have control over what I never had control over to begin with. I was able to rewrite my expectations, some of which were damn near impossible for anyone to meet, myself included, and others that were just silly. Nowadays, my husband and I are on the same page the majority of the time, but when we aren't, I understand that he is in control of himself. I can't make him do or be anything. I need to be open to his choices and willing to understand his reasoning behind them, especially when it doesn't match my own. I choose to love my husband unconditionally and see him with appreciation, even when his choice isn't my first pick. I seek to understand his perception and way of doing things, especially when they're different from my own. I love who he is as a person and have an unwavering respect for him. I give my husband the best gift of love by letting him be who he is and loving him no matter what. I understand that all of this is the only part that I can truly control.

So guess what, my friend?! You're off the hook too. You're not responsible for your husband's actions or lack thereof. You can only control and act for yourself. So when our husbands are doing something we don't understand or that we disagree with, it's not about how we can get them to change. It's about how we can love them anyway.

Let's be careful here, though. We aren't loving our husbands in spite of whatever we disagree with in an effort to manipulate them or put them in a position of "owing us" later on. We're loving our husbands simply because we love them. If you're doing something for someone so they can reciprocate, that's not a true act of love. But if you're doing something for someone because you know that will make them happy and you're happy to do it, that's love.

Might be a silly example, but whenever we would visit my husband's hometown in Brazil, he would always ask his mom to make beef tripe. This meal is one of his favorites, and he was always so happy when she would make it lovingly for him. I'm not a fan of this food at all, but out of love, I would smile and enjoy watching my husband's satisfaction in eating his favorite dish, even though it was always the worst lunch of the trip for me. My joy in that lunch was watching how happy my love was with his meal. I enjoyed seeing his mom's pride in giving her son one of his favorite foods and seeing the bond they had together. That was my satisfaction. My food during that lunch *sans* tripe was all right—nothing to write home about— but it didn't matter because of the joy that it brought to my husband.

Always Choose Love

Of course, my needs and wants matter too, but there are times, especially in marriage, that the biggest acts of love are when we put the other person's needs over our own. And please, before you go off on how it's a one-way street, and you always do that, but your husband *never* does, and it's just not fair, please stop and understand something. You always have a choice. You can always choose love. Getting defensive isn't going to get you where you want to be in your marriage. Getting mad by remembering all you do and what your husband doesn't do isn't going to get you there. Pointing out his shortcomings won't either. Take it back to that bigger perspective. How will *you* choose to act? How will *you* choose to love? It's time to realize your true power and embrace it. Your true power is in love—love for yourself, your husband, and your children.

These acts of love, when done consistently, will inspire those around you. Love is contagious. Isn't the best feeling in the world to be on the receiving side of a true act of love—something that someone does for you that you know they put thought and love into? And when that happens, don't you feel appreciative of the other person? Not because you have to but because you want to. It's good to feel loved. That's what we are all looking for—wives, husbands, and kids alike. Love evokes more love. In a true act of love, the person on the giving side isn't expecting anything in return but will be happy to receive as well. The importance here is in the expectation: there isn't one.

True love gives without keeping count. True love loves unconditionally. If you're supporting your husband and loving him unconditionally, he will love you unconditionally as well to the best of his ability. I know it's not all puppies and rainbows, and even in spite of unconditional love, every now and again the not-so-unconditional side of us pops up and wants to scream when things aren't happening a certain way. The more we make it a habit to be aware of our perceptions, how we're loving, and where our true control is, the better we become at it. Everything will become better in our lives as a result of this habit.

OK, fine, but how do I apply this IRL?

Realizing that I couldn't control my husband, even sometimes, was a tough pill for me to swallow. But seriously, once I got it, I was able to readjust my expectations, and my life went to a whole other level. It was easier to see my husband's perception and understanding, I could better relate to him, and we could come up with a solution that we both wanted. The choosing love part becomes easier with practice, but it's essential to understand where your husband is coming from to be able to choose love. Sometimes that looks like admitting, "I don't even know what is up with him" or "I don't even know where he is coming from." I encourage you to try to do the same. Try to realize that you can't control your significant other. Be more open to seeing his perception of things without taking offense to it. A lot of times, it will have very little to do with you anyway.

* How do I see my husband at this phase of our lives together?
* Is that how I want to feel about him?
* If no, what would I like to change about how I see him?
* What does he do that I find annoying?
* What could this be showing me about myself?
* What do I control?
* Am I really in control of these things, or is it just an illusion?
* Do I have to try to control this?

Embrace the Magic of Affirmations

* I am willing to see my husband in a new light.
* I take time to reflect on my beliefs, release what no longer serves me, and choose new perceptions.
* It's OK for things to be OK without me controlling them.
* I am safe. My family is safe.
* I choose to love instead of control.
* I accept my significant other.
* I choose to see my spouse with love.

CHAPTER 8

Talk to Me, Love

The third stressor related to husbands is such a big one that it deserves its own chapter. It's all about communication. One of the MOST common things I hear related to husbands is about communication or lack thereof. Girls, we know that communication is EVERYTHING! I'm not talking about nagging or complaining, "communicating" the to-do list, providing the daily update, or whatever. I'm talking about being clear and honest in what you expect of one another. The communication I'm talking about is just as much about listening as it is about talking.

After the first chapters of this book, I hope you're much clearer on what you need as a person and have taken an in-depth look at your expectations for yourself. Now, I encourage you to do the same for the expectations you have for your husband.

Communicate in a Loving Way

Once you get clearer on what you expect of your husband, communicate these expectations to him in a loving way in a moment when you are both in a good mood. This isn't something you should throw at him when you're annoyed because he's paying more attention to the rerun of *Pawn Stars* than your conversation. The best route is to find a time when you're both relaxed and bring it up calmly. Try to avoid saying things along the lines of "We really need to talk" or "I was thinking . . ." You can explain the work you have been putting into yourself and the thinking you have been doing to get clear on your expectations. Your husband will love to hear any discoveries you have made about where you have been wrong. I've found this is usually the best place to start. #thankmelater

For example, you could say, "I'm reading this book, and it's getting me to question some things. I'm kind of embarrassed to admit this, but I've been having unrealistic expectations of you. I want things to go a certain way, and when they don't, I get nasty. I didn't realize I was doing this until recently, so I'm sorry for the times I was a jerk to you inadvertently. It's something I'm working on. Anyway, it's really got me thinking about some important topics . . ." See how the conversation goes. It might go amazingly well, or it might be a giant disaster. Either way, don't worry! You can always try again and learn from your mistakes. Maybe you will unintentionally trigger your husband with a conversation like this. Collect that data and reassess for a better approach at a better time.

Please keep in mind that your husband, like anyone in the universe, has his own baggage and issues and sometimes can't be available for you the way you think he should be. You hope he will do his best, but for one reason or another, he could get weird when put in different situations, especially dealing with potentially heavy emotions.

> **Your husband can't give you what he doesn't have.**

His reaction is about him, not about you. Don't fall into his story of it being your fault or your responsibility. His stories are his. You get to decide what you believe and how you react. Your reaction will tell where you are in your story, just as much as his will determine where he is in his. Don't take it personally. Again, it's more about him than it is about you. If your husband is argumentative when approached, take a step back and evaluate the truth, if any, in his statements. There may be a lot of emotions attached to his statements, but by separating those, can you find some glimpses of truth? Is there a lesson in it for you? Is there anything you can work on? Hear him without bias. Take some time to reflect and get back to him. You can always say, "Thanks for sharing that with me. I'll take some time to think about it and try to apply what you are saying" or "This is new to me, so I'll need some time to process it, but thanks for telling me how you feel." Remember, you can't control how he feels, and he can't control your feelings either. Open communication can sometimes hurt and make us a little uncomfortable. Remember, you can always take a break if it's getting too heated and revisit it once everyone is calmer.

Try Not to Let Him Have It

I know how tempting it can be to list all of your grievances and really let your husband have it, because you are so fed up and tired of all of this stress (often, you think, because of him!). You think, "If he were me, he would understand!" But ladies, please know we would definitely be taking the wrong approach and not getting closer to the solution we so desperately want if we take this road.

> **We need to remember that it's our husbands and us against the issue, not us against our husbands.**

On my wedding day, I spoke my vows with an earnest hope that my brand-new husband and I would live happily ever after as a team, as partners, as best friends, in love forever. I would imagine this is the goal for everyone who gets married, right? They want to feel loved and be happy. No one gets married with the intent of living miserably ever after. In some of our darkest moments in marriage, what held my husband I together was remembering that we are one hell of a team. We're different in many ways, but those differences complement one another if we allow them to. Honestly, those differences are what give us our edge as a couple.

When we're irritated with one another, it takes some extra work to be loving, but if we resist our urge to complain, nag, or even to escape by calling friends, binge-watching TV, getting lost in social media, rage cleaning, or turning to food and instead change our focus and our approach, we'll be headed in the right direction—the direction of connection and love. Our whole goal in open communication is to voice our perceptions, to understand our husbands', and to find a mutually agreeable solution. We're in this together. We both want a happy life. We both deserve to be heard and understood.

It can be a slippery slope to bring up a sensitive topic to someone you love so much, especially when you're both in the thick of it. The most success I've had in doing so has been when using "I Statements." The use of I Statements is a powerful tool, created by Thomas Gordon, to communicate our feelings without intentionally blaming the person we're confronting. The structure is "I feel _____ when you _____ because _____. What I need is _____." These statements are great because they make the issue about us. It takes that blame off the other person. Remember, we aren't looking to make anyone feel bad or like an ass, even if we think they've been acting like one. We want our perception of the situation to be communicated clearly and effectively. If our husbands are receiving something that isn't as emotionally charged, they will be less likely to react in an overly defensive way, which means they may be more receptive to what we have to say.

Tips to navigate through this easily:

* Bring up the subject in an easy way.
* Do NOT say "we need to talk" or something else that indicates that hubby should take cover.
* Wait for a time when you're both relaxed and in a good mood.
* Do NOT let it rip when you're pissed off at him. To avoid doing this, you can say nothing at the time and reapproach a topic when you're calmer, or you can simply say, "I'm upset, angry, furious (whatever you are) now, and I need some time to process this and cool down."
* Use the sandwich technique. This is not to be confused with

bringing your husband a sandwich, although everything tends to go smoother when no one is hungry. The sandwich technique is when you start by saying something you appreciate about your man or something positive he does: "I really admire how well you worked with Alaina on her homework. You're great at explaining things in a way she can easily understand." Then you say what your issue is: "I've noticed, though, that there are times when she asks for your help, and you're distracted on your phone and don't answer her. I've noticed the same situation with me talking with you as well." Then you follow up with another genuine praise or positive comment for the last part of the sandwich: "I know you have a lot going on at work now and really appreciate all of the extra efforts you've been putting in there. I think you're a fantastic problem-solver, manager, negotiator, etc. All of your hard work will pay off soon. Our family is very lucky to have you.")

* Try to focus on the positive, bigger picture. Yes, you were annoyed at him, but for the most part, he is a wonderful partner. You did pick him, after all.

* Do NOT use sweeping statements like, "I always," "You never," or vice versa. Try to keep your focus on the behavior and not on your partner. The I Statements are lifesavers here.

Airing Your Concerns—Healthily

Many of the times I voice my concerns to my husband in our marriage, I've come to discover that the same issue I'm addressing is also bothering him to some degree. Sometimes it's in a different way, but airing our concerns is an eye-opening process for both of us. It helps us to collaborate on ideas to get us both closer to what we'd like for that given topic. We take the approach of "us versus the issue" rather than "him versus me," and it's so much more effective! Remember, you're in this thing together. You and your husband are a team. There are times in your marriage that one of you will give 90 percent and meet the other, who is only able to give 10 percent at that time. Other times it will be fifty-fifty, but it doesn't always have to be. The more flexible and adaptive this is in your marriage, the better it will be for both of you and everyone around you.

This is the perfect time for your husband and you to get clear on your expectations of one another. There's a chance your husband hasn't given this a lot of deliberate thought—what he expects of you as his wife, what he expects of himself as your husband and as a father to your kids. Please remember this is an ongoing process for life. We are always presented with new experiences and information with an opportunity to grow. This is something we will never finish fully. The best place to start is to get clear on what you want for yourself and then to ask what your husband would like for himself. Give him time to reflect on it. All of this doesn't need to be, nor can be, resolved in one day. It takes time. So instead of getting way ahead of yourself, please realize you can only focus on today.

You do need dreams and goals for the future, and you need to have an idea of where you're going, but you need to be more in the present. You need to hug more now. You need to kiss more now. You need to love more now. The present is where your power is. What are you doing now to spread love to yourself, your spouse, and your family?

OK, fine, but how do I apply this IRL?

I know it's not always easy to "be the bigger person," especially when you're annoyed AF. But like the majority of the nuggets of wisdom in this book, this too is like a muscle that will become stronger and easier to use over time if exercised. Practice makes better. Learning how to communicate your needs and expectations effectively and lovingly to your partner takes some trial and error. Learning how to receive his needs and expectations with compassion and love also takes practice. Your relationship is worth it, though. What the two of you get through together will make you better and stronger as a couple. If you can continue to grow and love one another in the beautiful chaos of parenting, you have the foundation to do anything together! Take a moment to reflect on the following questions about communication:

* In what ways am I voicing my needs?
* What are effective ways to share my needs with my significant other?
* What are ineffective ways to share my needs with him? Is there something I say or do that seemingly "shuts him off"?
* When my husband voices his side, do I take time to hear him out and reflect on what he's saying?
* Do I become defensive when he shares his views with me?
* What are the ways I prefer he share things with me?
* What method doesn't work for me?
* What would I like to see improve in communication with my spouse?
* What can I do to help that happen?

Embrace the Magic of Affirmations

* I am a wonderful communicator.
* I share my thoughts and ideas easily.
* I express my feelings openly with my spouse.
* I am a calm and receptive listener.
* I hear my partner out with patience and acceptance.
* I choose my words thoughtfully and express my ideas with grace.

CHAPTER 9

To Do's, To Be's and Not to Be's

The fourth stressor in marriage that we will discuss is getting too caught up in the to-do's of our lives. It's no secret that we have so much to do and seemingly little time to do it in (if that's our belief, right?). The tasks just keep coming, like Old Faithful. We get e-mails from the school about sock day and show-and-tell and the latest fundraiser—shit! I completely forgot I said I would donate cookies for tomorrow's bake sale. We have food and other things that we consume every day that need to be replaced. We keep tabs on our household inventory, on our adult wardrobes, clothes for the kids, the dry cleaning. We have chores on chores on chores to keep the house in a presentable state—or at least not too disgusting. We have carpools and playdates, birthday parties, and friends to check in on. We have appointments to coordinate and meetings to attend. If we don't stay on top of it all and schedule it in, we'll be rushed, unable to get as much done, or forgetting about the whole thing. And my oh my if that's not the truth!

Have you ever sat down for a minute and had this weird feeling you were forgetting something, only to discover that you were supposed to be someplace else at that very moment? I remember when my oldest son was in kindergarten. It was the Monday after Easter, and my younger son's daycare was closed that day. I was excited to have one more lazy morning, watching cartoons with the boys in the warm comfiness of my bed. I was thinking of fun things we could do together to enjoy this last

88

day of vacation. Right as I was ready to share an idea with the boys, my phone rang. It was the attendance office at my older boy's school. School was being held, and he was marked absent! Whaaaat?! Who has school the Monday after Easter? Umm, apparently our district does. So I mad dashed it, and we were there as quickly as possible. On the way to school, I realized it was April 1, so we were at least able to laugh about it, but I had no idea there was school because it wasn't marked on my personal calendar. Rookie mistake. But we've all been there.

The Power of Reminiscing

There's an onslaught of stuff to do every single day, and, if we aren't careful, we get sucked into the chaotic whirlwind of go, go, go, and do, do, do. We can easily lose sight of what's most important to us. We love our families. We love our husbands, and we love ourselves. But there's so much that happens in our day-to-day that seems so urgent, so we put it ahead of our highest priorities. Our mom alarm is continually going off. *Help! Help! Help!* We need it, and we have people who need it from us! We slip into a reactive mode and lose our connection with ourselves. The best way to get around this very common stressor of the nonstop to-do list and prevent getting sucked into the hectic-ness of that is to plan a time (or multiple times) during your day for fun and things that help you keep it light.

One way to help us keep things in a favorable perspective, especially regarding our husbands, is to reminisce. I'm sure we can all remember the pre-kid days, even though we can't imagine our lives without our kiddos now. In those days, we did what we wanted, when we wanted. If we wanted to hop in the car and take an impromptu trip, we did. If we wanted to lounge around all day long, watching movies with spicy lovemaking in between, we did. We only had ourselves to answer to. It was glorious! I remind myself that it wasn't just about the freedom, but it was about the undivided love and attention my husband and I could give one another. I didn't ever have to wait until later to discuss something pressing with him. The to-do list didn't seem as urgent. There weren't as many schedules to coordinate and fewer restrictions. It was an amazing phase.

I like to remember this phase often, as I find part of my current sanity there. I loved my husband first. All of what we have together today started way back then. I love our love that we have built our family on. I smile in gratitude when I think of our family and life together—you know, the "all because two people fell in love" idea. It's remarkable and oh so fun to think back to those "simpler times," especially in the hecticness of our life now with three kids. I laugh as I remember thinking I had so much to do and so little time to do it or how exhausted I felt. Not to take anything away from that, of course! It was true for me at the time. I was busy, and I was exhausted, but that version of Stephanie couldn't do what my current version can by a long shot. It makes me appreciate who I have become and realize how much I'm able to do. I love to look back and see my growth, my husband's growth, and the ways we've grown together. Not only is it fun to look back over old photographs and remember things from a simpler time, but it brings a new level of clarity to my current reality. I reconnect with what I loved most about my husband in those times, which makes what I love about him now stronger too. Reminiscing is essential for my marriage. It helps me stay in touch with the bigger picture and keep that spark alive and burning strong. Give it a try for yourself and see what it can do for you.

In All Seriousness, Don't Be So Serious (All the Time)

The fifth stressor in our marriages nicely piggybacks on the fourth: **We take ourselves and our lives too seriously.** When we're too caught up in the hustle and bustle of this beautiful chaos of motherhood, it's easy to take things too seriously. We forget that it's essential to have fun. After all, what else is life about? Let's not lose touch with our joy. We can easily turn into sour apples, like the guy on the expressway who grumpily passed by the busload of kids, wildly pumping their arms up and down, asking for him a quick honk, and who disappointed them all. If we choose to behave that way, we'll most likely have a stinky remainder of the day.

One of the best antidotes for taking ourselves too seriously is to find the humor in any given situation. I enjoy doing this to keep my mind right when the craziness of life creeps in. Like anything, this is a habit that needs to be developed. It can seem hard at first when you aren't used to looking for fun or humor. It's been said that the best medicine is laughter, right? If you can't laugh at yourself and with your partner at the sometimes wacky and eyebrow-raising situations of life, what are you even doing? Things go easier and become more enjoyable when we're having fun. As you embrace the chaos and go within to find your peace, you naturally allow more joy into your life and into your relationships.

And while you cannot ever, ever, ever make anyone change, you can always inspire others with a good attitude. It's so much easier to shine as brightly as you can when you're on that upward spiral. Humor, related to the present moment or not, always helps to get you headed in that direction. Sometimes at the end of a long day, or even in the middle of it, I'll take a break from what I'm working on and pull up some videos on YouTube that will get me laughing and lighten my mood. My personal faves are the hashtag videos from *The Tonight Show Starring Jimmy Fallon*, anything Michael McIntyre, and the YouTube channel *Juggling the Jenkins*. When I can't readily laugh during my day-to-day hustle, I know I need a quick time-out to lighten up. There are times I look for cake-decorating videos to soothe me and times I look for comic relief, online or in real life. If I'm paying attention, my kids can be downright hilarious. My spouse is fun, and we love laughing together. If either of us is in a funk and not so easily amused, sometimes a good thing to try is a change of environment. Get out of the house or change the dynamic by inviting a friend over or calling someone.

What else can you do? You can put on your favorite music and dance around. If you focus on keeping your mood light, you can be influential to your family as well. Just like love, joy is also contagious. It's important to remember that you don't have to be so serious. You can have fun while you work on even the most mundane tasks. Work, chores, and any other activity is better when you're easy about it and enjoy the potential fun in the moment.

Running jokes are also priceless. One of our go-to's is from when my son, William, got braces. He and his brother started roughhousing with one another as per usual, and William would get nervous if his brother was being too strong (in other words, if his brother was winning the wrestling match) and would say, "Chill, Michael, I have braces." Since my boys love to wrestle and live a life of full-contact, we heard this phrase often. Now any time something becomes too heated in or out of the home, one of us will say, "Chill, I have braces," and the mood lightens. So think of the silly situations that you and your family have lived that you can bring into your tense moments to lighten them up.

Nothing Compares to You, Mamacita

Our next weedy marriage stressor is comparison. Like the axiom so beautifully explains, "comparison is the thief of joy." Well, honey, it's also the thief of a happy marriage. Don't believe me? Just hop on social media and see your friend's husband cooking a delicious meal, doing a beautiful home remodeling project, or basking in the sun with his love while you and your beau aren't doing any of those things. Not to mention how husbands are often portrayed in film—I'm looking at you, Noah Calhoun (from *The Notebook*)! In these moments of comparison, we get into a dangerous place. Similar to those unrealistic expectations we set for ourselves and our loved ones, comparison of our husband to another's is a landmine.

Intellectually, we know each person has his or her special talents and gifts. Some people are wonderful artists, some are master chefs, some are handy, and some are extra hilarious. We will never find two people who offer the exact same skill set to the world. When we compare and focus on what our husband is *not* doing, we're closing our eyes to the parts that he *is* doing and failing to recognize his talents. We're most likely to compare our husbands to someone else's in an area that we're not satisfied with.

I found this to be true for myself when my sons were two and one. I was overworked and stressed to the max. Having the boys only fourteen months apart left me frazzled and in over my head. I didn't know about self-care or not being able to fill from an empty cup. I was running on fumes. I didn't voice this to anyone, partly because I didn't know and partly because I didn't feel like I had the right to do so because I was a stay-at-home mom at the time (more on that later). I would fantasize about silly things, like an uninterrupted trip to the bathroom, sleeping in, or not being at anyone's beck and call 24/7. There were many meals that I barely tasted because I was feeding my toddler while calming my baby, and by the time everyone else was fed and appeased, dinner was done. So I would either sit alone to eat my cold food or just call it a wrap and get on with the next part of the schedule. My husband was there, and he was interested in supporting me, but since I didn't tell him what was bothering me, it never dawned on him to offer help. He thought I had it under control, which I kind of did on the surface, but at the price of my inner sanity. So when my brother-in-law and sister-in-law would come over for dinner, and my brother-in-law would anticipate my need for help, it was such a breath of fresh air. Instead of realizing that my husband didn't even notice what was going on, let alone that it was bothering me, I ended up taking the easy way out and sulking in my dissatisfaction instead of telling him how I felt.

I compared my husband to my brother-in-law, thinking things like, "Ugh, why can't he be more like him?! It is so helpful to have someone who notices and acts to help." Then I would get mad at my husband, never voicing it, though, for not getting it. That was a big, fat weed in my marriage that almost choked us out. My comparison didn't let me enjoy the things that my husband *was* doing right at the time. He is an excellent dad, and his boys love him dearly. He plays with them and gets the best giggles from them. He always has the best ideas for activities that the boys adore. He is affectionate and fun to be around. My comparison blinded me from those good points for a long time. I became resentful, yet I still didn't talk about it. I was focused on what I didn't like about my husband, which probably could have easily been handled with a conversation or two. I didn't choose that way, and it cost me a lot of grief and trouble.

This area of dissatisfaction tainted the other areas of my marriage. It is easy to have this happen in even the best marriages. With the widespread use of social media, there are opportunities to compare ourselves and our husbands to others with each scroll. Now, with my years of wisdom and experience in this area, I know if I find myself scrolling through social media and comparing a friend's husband to mine (or comparing any part of her life to mine), I know there's something there for me to investigate. Why is this a trigger for me? What is this about? What does it represent in my life? How do I feel about this area? Is there a better way to see this situation? Is there something I can work on in my own life to change the way I see this?

The best example I have of this was several years ago when I was talking with a friend, and she mentioned that she and her husband were taking a trip, just the two of them, to some cool, exotic place that I had always dreamed of going. I was puzzled because her kids were the same age as mine, and she had just had her third baby. I had just had mine as well. Please keep in mind, this was before my therapy and the healing of many areas of my life. I started judging my friend and her husband and comparing their lives with ours, thinking things like, "They must be happier than we are, they must have more money than we do, they must not care about their kids as much as we do." This situation was one that came up repeatedly in my energy work with my therapist, and it was a doozy for me.

My intense negative emotions and judgments were an obvious indicator of my huge issue with this topic. I didn't have a problem with the fact that my friends were traveling and enjoying their lives. I had a problem with what was ruffled up in my own life at the thought of this. I had no idea I had major issues in leaving my kids in someone else's care. I was not OK with trusting someone else to take care of them. So my friend's liberty in traveling alone with her husband irritated many wounds of my past that were unhealed. I didn't understand how she could leave her children when I couldn't leave mine. I didn't understand how they could justify the cost of the trip while they were responsible for these little people, solely based on my limiting beliefs that there wasn't enough money to do everything I wanted at the time. I believed that it had to be one or the other. I simply couldn't have it all. I certainly didn't understand her excitement about any of this, either. It was hard for me to fake my enthusiasm for her, but now I understand that each part of this situation was an indicator of my many limiting beliefs that needed to be reworked at the time.

Fast-forward several years. I've taken a trip away with my husband for the past three years, one of them being a three-week trip to Thailand and China. I'm happy to report that the trip was incredible, and I was at peace about the whole thing the entire time. So what was the difference between how I felt about my friend's trip and my recent trips? I had the chance to rework my beliefs and heal my past issues. My inner comparison to my friend and her husband was my first sign that there was work that needed to be done. At the time, it stole my joy. It also caused me to see myself and my husband in a negative light. I was depressed and felt trapped. But with therapy and a willingness to change, I was able to overcome these self-imposed obstacles and rise higher, enjoying myself and my husband more than ever. So if you find yourself saying something like, "Sarah's husband always helps with the chores and gives the baths, likes to dance, is affectionate, etc.," please realize that this is an opportunity to dive deep and figure out what's missing for you on a given topic.

When you're comparing your husband (or kids or even yourself) to anyone else and expecting him to be like that other person, you may think you're focusing on what you like about the other person. It may not seem that bad, right? While I'm comparing how much time my friend's husband spends with his child to how much my husband spends with our child, or how much the other person helps out with chores or whatever, I might think that I'm focusing on helping out with chores or spending time with kids. Sounds kind of positive, but don't be fooled! It's not positive at all. The energy behind this thought is a focus on what your husband is NOT doing. It's seeing a lack, and from that place, you can't find the joy, love, and appreciation. You block yourself from seeing what he's doing well.

Every couple has its own dynamic. Every couple has its own system for what works and what doesn't work. It's extremely unique. There are very few things that are the same across the board for all couples. Comparison, then, shouldn't be used as a measure of performance for either person in a relationship. Each one should be admired for his or her strengths and positive attributes. Nothing is accomplished by comparing your loved ones to someone else. You might ask whether it's OK to compare to inspire another to be better. Well, that's a good thought; however, it's very difficult to do this in a way that will be perceived as coming from a place of love.

When I was first married, my husband would innocently compare me to his best friend's wife, who was a speed-cleaning organization goddess. I was more sloth-like and indifferent in my cleaning attempts. His intention was to inspire me to learn from her amazing example, but that didn't happen. It had the reverse effect on me. I raised an eyebrow, copped an attitude, and was purposefully slower. Even worse, I questioned my husband's loyalty to me and felt like he regretted picking a messy, slow-cleaning wife.

Plain and simple, comparison is a bitch. When we aren't comparing ourselves and husbands to others, we can fall into the trap of comparing ourselves *to* our husbands. We compare who wakes up earlier, who works harder, who does more of the shitty parts of parenting and who gets to do more of the glamorous parts, and who receives the most recognition. And so on and so on. If we aren't careful and in tune with what's working and making us feel good and what isn't working and making us feel depleted, we'll internalize these comparisons in the form of resentment and grudges.

Take the dinner dishes, for example. I have a love-hate relationship with the dishes, depending on how I perceive that task on any given day. There are times I put on music or an audiobook, and the job is almost therapeutic. Then there are other times that I feel trapped because I ALWAYS do the dishes, whereas my husband never does. I then begin to compare the number of chores that I consistently do to what he doesn't do, and I get angry. I get resentful, and it all goes to shit. I'm not in a place of appreciation for my husband or even myself at that point. In those moments, I'm choosing to ride the wave of complaining and comparing. I can usually talk myself down from this ledge by pointing out that our marriage and our dynamic isn't a competition. It's not who does what, but how we feel doing it.

I ask myself important questions regarding what will make me feel better doing a task. What do I need? What can I do to change this crappy perspective? I know my husband and I are different and have different roles that we play in our lives. Sometimes we take turns doing those roles, and sometimes we stick to what we do best. It's our dynamic, and the most important thing is that it works for us. Comparing my tasks, input, output, etc. to my husband's is a waste of time. Let's remember—it's us as a team against the issue, not us against one another. There is simply no room for comparison in marriage!

OK, fine, but how do I apply this IRL?

The three stressors we talked about in this chapter can dominate our minds if we let them. Each one amplifies the next and puts even more pressure on us as moms. We can get too caught up in all we have to do, take ourselves too seriously, and cut ourselves off from fun, which can start the vicious cycle of comparison. Sprinkle these into the jam-packed days of beautiful chaos, and it's an automatic shit show with no easy exit in sight. Any time you feel yourself getting swept away by any of these stressors, grab on to the branches in this chapter to stay afloat. To take a deeper look at each of these areas, ask yourself the following:

* What parts of my life have become routine?
* What can I do to change these things?
* What would make them more enjoyable?
* What are some things that always make me laugh?
* How can I bring these things into my daily routine?
* Can I give myself permission to take a few minutes to laugh and lighten up during the day?

* What are the ways I compare my husband to others?
* What are other ways comparison is affecting my marriage?

Embrace the Magic of Affirmations

* I find joy in daily activities.
* I look for ways to have fun and enjoy each moment of my day.
* I reflect on happy memories from my past with my significant other.
* I love remembering how we loved each other in every stage of our relationship.
* I look for ways to laugh and relax throughout my day.
* I love laughing and feeling good.
* I know I have a better time when I am relaxed.
* When I find myself comparing, I make a choice to focus on what I appreciate about my husband.
* I am enough. My husband is enough. My marriage is enough.
* I am thankful for this life we have together.

CHAPTER 10

Appreciation Goes Both Ways

When we're busting our butts to do as much as we possibly can for our families, and we don't feel appreciated, it's one of the most disheartening feelings *ever*. It's a real downer. We can be left to wonder what the point of all of this BS really is. Seriously, why do all of this just to be taken for granted? We've probably all felt this way. We all know how badly it stinks.

However, we can turn this into a lesson for learning to feel good emotions. We need to remember this feeling and ask ourselves who *we* are taking for granted and who *we* are unintentionally making feel this way. The people most at risk for this type of treatment are often those closest to us, the people we see and have the most interaction with.

Continuing with our discussion of marital stressors in the previous chapter, **the next major stressor is a lack of appreciation.** Appreciation goes both ways, right? Of course, it's crucial for us to feel appreciated, but more important is for us to appreciate those around us, because that is something we can actually control. Life with our loved ones can become automatic without us even realizing it. We need to be careful to avoid this trap.

Lack of appreciation is one of the biggest stressors in a marriage. And while we all know that the simplest solution is to show appreciation, that can be harder than it sounds, depending on our situation. Our husbands are an excellent place to start! If we're working on our inner peace, we will be in a place where it's easier for us to find what we admire and value about our husbands. Appreciation is most easily accessed when we are in a good place mentally and emotionally. Music, humor, and reminiscing are all ways to get to a better-feeling place where it's easier to find our appreciation of our spouses. We can also find it from a not-so-good place, but we will probably have to do a little more work to get there. Here's a universal truth bomb:

> **It's impossible to be in a state of appreciation while criticizing. It's impossible, absolutely impossible, to feel a lot of love for someone, no matter who they are, from a place of criticizing and complaining about them.**

Make Appreciation a Habit

We know our thoughts and expectations are habits. We can always choose what we think and expect at any given moment. Well, appreciation is a habit that we need to bring our attention to, especially regarding the perception of our husbands. Maybe you're in a good habit of running through a daily list of things that you admire and appreciate about him. Maybe you are in the habit of focusing on his flaws and shortcomings, and you may not have even noticed you're doing so before reading this. The best thing about bad habits is that they can change. It takes awareness, desire, and persistence. Take a minute to think about this next question: Do you find yourself saying more positive or negative things about your husband (thinking positive or negative thoughts counts too!)? If you aren't sure, take the next twenty-four hours and bring your awareness to how you view your husband—thoughts you think, statements you make, the way you talk to him, the tone you use when talking to him, and the way you talk about him to others. Then ask yourself if you found more positives or negatives. What comment/thought/tone surprised you the most? How would you feel being on the receiving end of this?

Once we become aware of our habitual ways of perceiving our husbands, we can focus on shifting them as needed. Our appreciation of our best friend and soulmate is essential to the growth of our love and the health of our marriage. Let's go back to our example several chapters back of the husband who slept in *again* and is now napping, leaving the wife to fend for herself and the kids. She's probably super irritated. I know we can all relate to this. I know we have all been in a situation like this at some point during motherhood. If the wife in the example is in the habit of criticizing her husband, the day will end in flames. She won't find her appreciation in that moment, and all bets are off for a good weekend. If she's in the habit of appreciation, she'll have an easier time being gracious and understanding her husband's side. The fury and flames will most likely be avoided.

Let's be clear: I'm not saying that if the wife appreciated her husband more he could then go and do whatever the hell he wants. But I *am* saying that husbands will do annoying things—guaranteed. And wives will do annoying things too—guaranteed. The momentum we create around our spouses will determine how we perceive their annoyingness. Think of it as a bank account, and each irritating act is a debit. If we aren't actively making it a point to deposit good feelings in the account, we'll get angrier and increasingly annoyed with each debit until the account is completely depleted. Appreciation is the best way to deposit into your account. It goes hand in hand with love, and the more you have of one, the more you will have of the other.

We've all been right in the thick of things in our day-to-day lives, which are full of mundane tasks and routines. Same thing, different day, and our husbands are there at their usual times, and things become routine, kind of blah, even. There's no more "can't wait to get home to see him" urgency or "can't keep your hands off of one another" passion. There is "we love one another more than ever at this point because of everything we've been through together," but it's easy to begin to take our husbands for granted. If we aren't consciously refining our perspectives of our husbands, it becomes easier to see what he didn't do than what he did because we're so used to him doing the things that he does. The same goes for him—he's used to us doing our tasks as well and may not value it as much as he did in the beginning. When a marriage is like this, the relationship needs a breath of fresh air. In this case, that breath is in the form of appreciation. Make a habit of appreciating your husband, daily or weekly, but please consider *often* the aspects that you appreciate about him. The more often you practice this, the better you will be at it, and the more easily the list will flow. If you're currently mad at your husband and find it challenging to get a list going of things you appreciate about him now, maybe you need to zoom out a little and go to a time when he was easier to appreciate, even if that means going waaaay back. We all have a time that we easily appreciated our man, even if it was in the very beginning.

Here are some questions to get you headed in the right direction with your appreciation:

* What do you admire about your husband?
* What are some things he has done that have really impressed you?
* What are you thankful for about him?
* What amazes you about him?
* What are some of the qualities you fell in love with and continue to fall in love with?

Now, as you build this practice into your day or week, allow your level of love for your man to increase. It will be easier to show your love to him in every way. The more love you feel, the more attracted you will be to him, and the more appealing he will become to you. Your showing that love to him will be the start of him recognizing his love for you in a new way. Think about it: when you know someone appreciates you, you stop whatever you're doing and notice them. You appreciate them back. Appreciation will defibrillate your life. It will bring you to new heights. Your relationship will improve, which will give you more to appreciate, and so on and so forth. We talked about the idea of changing your perception of your husband, especially if you happen to be in a pattern of focusing on what he does (or doesn't do) that irritates you. Since we know we can't be in a place of complaining and loving simultaneously, we need to practice our appreciation of our husbands on the daily so we're naturally inclined to do so.

The best exercise for this is to get some paper and make some lists:

* Things I appreciate about my husband (attributes he has that I love, admire, or am thankful for)
* Things I appreciate about our relationship (things that we do together, are together, or have together)
* Ways my husband has influenced my life (ways that he has positively contributed and continues to contribute to your life)

As you identify these traits, be sure to get clear on what a successful marriage is as well. What does it look like to you? The clearer you become on this, the easier time you will have in identifying strategies with your husband to get you both there. Listen to his ideas of a successful marriage. What does it look like for him? What does he appreciate about your marriage now?

It's OK to Be Annoyed (and Annoying)

Please understand that your husband will still do things that annoy you or that you would rather he didn't do, and you will continue to do the same for him, no matter how much he adores you. It's a fact of life, and once we embrace this reality that people will annoy us from time to time, our lives become a little more satisfying. It becomes easier for us to realize the good. While it's an enormous step to focus on what you admire about your husband, be sure to make room for that appreciation to continue. Don't allow old habits of critiquing or complaining about him (even if it's just to yourself and never said aloud) to creep back in. Complaints are weeds that will spread and dominate your garden of marriage.

We need to come from a place of love if we want *any* type of progress. Passive-aggressive or sarcastic tactics will only worsen the issue at hand, creating more strife and bad vibes. How can we be loving when we're so freakin' irritated?! Well, to put it simply, we can't. What we can do, though, is recognize our irritation and move through it to a better-feeling place, all the way up to love.

Not that any of this is easy, but when you find yourself in that irritated state, remember this little secret—I'm pretty sure I speak for all husbands when I say that you will get more from them with a nice approach than a bitchy one. Here's why: the same way you have needs and want to feel loved and appreciated, so does your husband. Many times, as women, we have the emotional know-how to recognize this, often before our husbands. Knowledge is power, and we need to use this knowledge to help our marriages. I know my husband wants to feel appreciated. I know he wants to feel loved. I know he does his best every day (even if there are times it leaves me SMH saying WTF under my breath). I know that I do my best every day too, even on those days that aren't so great. I want to feel the same as my man does as well. How can I show him my appreciation if I'm focusing on what he's doing wrong? How much of what he does do I take for granted? Before we flip the script and ask the same questions of him and his actions, take a second to answer these questions honestly:

* What am I doing on the daily to appreciate, compliment, or love my husband?
* Does he know how much he means to me?
* What are some ways that I have shown him these things this month? This week? Today?

**Appreciation is the FIRST MAJOR KEY
in a successful marriage.**

Appreciation Goes Both Ways   105

If you're continually looking for what you appreciate in your mate, you'll have an easier time in the inevitable "irritating" moments, but more importantly, you'll truly value the love of your life in deeper and more meaningful ways.

Feeling Lonely Amid the Chaos

Our next stressor, feeling like we are in this all alone, is inevitable when we're not making appreciation a priority in our marriage. This is exactly why we need to discuss this one in depth. Based on a survey I conducted, one in three mothers claims she doesn't have enough help from her husband, which is a great source of daily stress. We moms are stressed about the lack of time to get everything done. Seventy-nine percent of mothers I surveyed report that they do the majority of the household and parenting duties, as well as carrying most of the emotional load of the family. Parenting is intuitive for us moms; it just comes so naturally. Most of the time, I already know why my daughter is upset or why my son is in a funk. Moms are the ones always tuned in to the family's happenings. Being kick-ass multitaskers is a blessing and a curse for us moms. We can be in the kitchen making dinner and fully aware of the dispute happening in the living room over the blue Wii controller, so that when inevitably our child comes in and is upset, we not only already know what's coming, but we're armed with the best way we know for how to mediate the situation. This is the biggest reason moms can't sleep on the couch like dads. I marvel at the ease of my husband to drift off to sleep peacefully on the sofa in spite of the conversations, play, and squeals swirling around him. It's something I truly admire about him and have always been secretly jealous of. I know, however, that I'm wired differently, so I've given up on my nap dreams, at least while everyone is home and buzzing around.

I really learned what this meant in December of 2017, when I discovered that I needed to get surgery due to a bone issue that was causing a lot of pain in my foot. I remember the mixed emotions when the podiatrist told me the recovery would involve being completely off of my left foot for three weeks. He said that the more I rested, the quicker my recovery would be. I laughed and told him I had three kids—and it was December! One of the busiest months for me. Naturally, there were lots of things going through my mind at hearing his medical advice. Part of me was excited by this idea—yes! Vacation, finally!! I felt like I was off the hook in some ways. Another part of me was freaked out and downright overwhelmed by all I would have to prepare ahead of time for things to flow smoothly during those weeks of recovery. I was thinking of that list from chapter 1 multiplied by a hundred thanks to extra holiday events with three different schools, the Elf on the Shelf every effing night, and being Santa's right-hand lady for three ever-changing lists! Seriously, what's up with no one knowing what they *really* want for Christmas until the week before?!

In the moments after leaving the podiatrist's office, I realized how much I do for my family, for the house, for our lives—especially during the holidays. I was in awe and appreciation and also in a state of shock. Like any rational woman, my mind fast-forwarded to the worst possible scenario, and I was terrified. If something were to happen to me, how would my family survive? Would they know how to do things for themselves? Would they ever be able to find half of their belongings? There is so much behind-the-scenes work that goes into any given week in my family's life, let alone the most wonderful time of the year.

My children were ten, nine, and three at the time. The older two were used to helping out with minor chores (clearing the table and emptying the dishwasher), and the youngest was chore-free. Would my husband be up for the task at hand? (Well, not like he had a choice, but I was anxious to see how this would all play out.) I knew this was a time for me to learn how to rest and to refocus on myself. It made perfect sense to me that it was during one of the most hectic times of the year—seriously, the Universe has such a hilarious sense of humor.

My mental state going into this time was one of ease and stillness. The greatest lesson I learned during this experience, other than what wonderful exercise crutches can provide and that a kid's winter hat can add extra insulation on that oh-so-flattering post-op boot, is that it all works out, one way or another. When I was "forced" to back down, guess what? My family stepped up! Things still got done! They actually got done with less stress and craziness than normal in some cases. I thoroughly enjoyed the experience of seeing my family members step up and shine, using their gifts and contributing to our family.

So learn from me and this experience—you don't need your own surgery to take you out of commission to benefit from this lesson. It's perfectly OK to step back and delegate some of your workload. You're not in this alone, even though it may seem that way. I was used to doing the majority of things myself because I didn't imagine that my family could do what I do the way I do it. I always thought it was easier to just do it myself than to explain how to do it or point out what needed to be done. I didn't want to nag anyone, and I didn't want to spend energy that way. I would've rather used the energy to just do the damn thing. During my downtime, I focused a lot of my expectations and realized that if I didn't back off, there was no reason for my family to step up. Ever. Now's a great time to get clear on what you expect from yourself, your husband, and your kids. It's crucial that this is a conversation you have together!! Otherwise, you could just be setting everyone up for failure.

I was hugely guilty of this in my earlier years of marriage. I would make all of these plans and have these ideas of what my husband should be doing and what we would do together that weekend, except I wouldn't tell him. I'm not really sure if I thought I married a mind reader or not, but it was guaranteed that he would not do whatever it was I had dreamed up, and then I would get mad—at him! How silly! I have to laugh about it now because it sounds absurd. Nowadays, I rarely put myself in that situation, but if I do, I get frustrated—not with him, but with myself. If I'm not clear on my expectations, or worse, if I'm not realistic in my expectations, I will be frustrated, but almost always at my own miscalculation.

It's OK that my husband steps up and plays to his strengths. Ask my family—they'll tell you that cooking is not my strongest gift. But man, can my husband cook! I am one lucky woman to have such a wonderful chef in my life! You know those people who cook from their hearts? That's my man! He will cook for us and is happy to do so (and so is everyone else at the table!!). I gladly have relinquished my "duty" of cooking to my husband, because he's better at it. That's not to say that I never cook, but we've found what works best for us, so he cooks as much as he can. Same with household repairs—I *could* do them, but it's easier for him, so that's his thing too.

I highly recommend that each member of your household utilize their strengths. My oldest son, William, has an easy time with technology. My aunt explains that this is due to the fact that kids are born with USB cables in place of umbilical cords nowadays, but anyway. I *could* figure out the tech issue eventually, with several YouTube tutorials and a couple of calls to customer service, but it's so easy for William that fixing tech issues has become his role for the time being in our home. It feels good to be part of a family and help out by using your strengths. You'll be helping everyone in your life by sharing the load. You're only one person, and it's not a fair expectation of yourself to think you can do it all. If you don't give some room for your family members to step up and help, they won't. I mean, think about it, would you do the dishes if you really didn't *have* to? Like if you had a child or spouse who did the dishes before you could get to it and never complained about it, would you insist that you do the dishes? Of course not!! Our families don't step up because they have no idea that they should have, would have, could have.

An important note on being a recovering perfectionist: I know how challenging it can be to want things done a certain way and to get frustrated when they aren't completed in exactly that way by a family member. In fact, I know how it is to be so frustrated that you kick yourself for ever thinking that delegating work would be possible and miserably accepting the fact that you'll be doing everything until the end of time. Well, girlfriend, to that I say, "Get over yourself!" There are more ways than one to do any task. Maybe it was the post-op pain meds, but when I was laid up on the couch with my foot throbbing in the air and the dishes needing done, I couldn't have cared less! I saw my son loading the dishwasher in a very different way from my particular system and didn't give a rip. It was getting done, and it was working out. The how didn't matter. Keeping the bigger picture in mind, how the dishwasher is loaded doesn't make a difference whatsoever in my life. I can loosen my systematic grip on that one. Variety is the spice of life after all, right? And with some rewiring, you'll be able to rewrite these beliefs, and it will become easier for you to allow others to help.

If you take a loving approach, you can teach a family member how you would like a task to be done, but please remain open to their ideas. You may be surprised to see they found a better or more efficient way. Allow yourself to question your routines and habits. Allow the other person to enrich your life with new ways of doing something. Does it really matter what way your son chooses to fold his laundry as long as the end goal of having clean, non-wrinkly clothes that are easy to find and ready to wear is met? Does it really make a difference if your husband enjoys a chore more doing it his way than doing it your way as long as the end product is achieved? Does it matter if he completes this task in the morning or in the afternoon, or even the next day? Be really honest with yourself on these questions and be open to allowing change.

You may end up pleasantly surprised when you share some of your load. My son Michael discovered a game-changing life hack that my family has fully adopted as a result of his being given a task that was left completely up to him. He had to take out the trash and wound up with a brilliant idea. A pet peeve my husband and I share is someone taking out the trash bag without replacing it. I mean, it's the worst when you have a goopy mess that you go to throw away, and there's no bag in the can. Ugh, so gross and mega-frustrating! So my son created this magnificent idea to layer the trash bags. He put one trash bag in the trash can as normal, then opened another and put it over the first in the trash can and repeated this a few more times. There was a total of five or six bags ready to go. When we fill up the top one, the person on trash duty will pull it out and take it to the garage and be free to go about their normally scheduled day. They don't have to remember to come back to the kitchen to replace the bag. Boom! Our lives have changed for the better!

OK, fine, but how do I apply this IRL?

Something that I've heard just about every wife say at one point or another about their marital relationship is, "I feel like it's always on me. I feel like I'm always the one who has to _____." The fill-in-the-blanks have ranged from admitting wrongdoing first, bearing the emotional load, and processing feelings to doing whatever no one else wants to do because otherwise, it won't get done.

Well, this might be very annoying to you, but try to see the beauty and blessing in this next statement. We (women, wives, moms, sisters, friends, daughters, females) have chosen this role for a reason. We are here because we are lighthouses. I'm not saying that women are superior or inferior, but I am saying that we have special and natural gifts and talents that help in being the lighthouse in our family's universe. I've heard it said that when the mom leaves the home, the light goes out for that time. Sure, that might be a little extreme, but I point this out to illustrate the fact that you can see this as an annoyance ("Ugh, it's always me who has to analyze the situation and walk everyone else through" or "I'm always the one to initiate appreciation" or "When is my husband going to make his gratitude list? He's more negative than I am. He needs this more") or an opportunity. It can be tough to embrace our role. It can be uncomfortable. It can be scary and unnerving. But when we fully embrace our role as a lighthouse to ourselves, our partners, and our children, it can be magical. It can be amazing. It can be miraculous. So really go back to focusing on not keeping people on the hook for what they are or aren't doing.

Remember, you are the ONLY one who you can control. Choose appreciation over complaints, love over judgments, compassion over unrealistic expectations. Choose to be the light of your universe. You will be the one to benefit the most from this, but your husband, children, and everyone else around will benefit as well. Your light will be an unspoken example to those dearest to you, and they will be inspired. They will have an easier time finding their own light and shining bright because of you and your example. Consider the following questions for more clarity:

* What do I appreciate about myself?
* What do I appreciate about my husband?
* How can I show him I appreciate these things?
* Does he know how much I admire these things?
* Is there a deeper issue for me when I feel like I'm in this all alone?
* Is there something preventive I could do to change this?
* Do I need to ask for help?
* What are the ways I can get the support and help I need?

Embrace the Magic of Affirmations

* I take time each day to list what I most admire about my husband.
* I am thankful for my husband and our lives together.
* It's OK to feel annoyed. I recognize it and question it to see if there's something deeper for me. If not, I let it go with love.
* I am a creative problem solver, and there is always a solution.
* I always have everything that I need.
* I am supported and loved.
* I take time for myself so I can be a better woman.

CHAPTER 11

Love and Sex:
Handle It Like a Goddess

We have established that appreciation is the first major key in marriage; the second is love. **Another huge and very common stressor in marriage is lack of love or not feeling "in love" anymore.** You know, when you look at your spouse and think, "Oh, shit! How did we get *here?*" There are songs about this. There are movies, sitcoms, and all the real-life examples we witness with friends, family, and our own experiences. I bet we all know at least one couple who has slowly, over time, lost that loving feeling. This situation creeps up slowly and subtly. It sneaks into our marriages, right under our noses.

The best analogy of this problem is a garden. The prettiest gardens have someone out there in them every day. They're weeding, watering, observing, and doing whatever is necessary to keep the garden as beautiful as possible. In the rare moment when no work is needed, the gardener is still there to admire the beauty and the gorgeously maintained plants. He or she is present and has the intention of doing whatever it takes to keep the garden as beautiful as possible. The garden is for its keeper's enjoyment, and this person views it with the highest regard. But what happens when a garden's neglected?

Let's Talk S-E-X

In our gardens of love, when I say that love is the second key of marriage, of course I'm talking about the "I love you with my whole being" side of love and even the "have the last piece of cake because I know it's your favorite" love. I'm also referring to the physical love: ahem—sex. For most of us, physical intimacy with our husbands, namely our sex life, is the first thing to go when life comes knocking, especially life with kids. We may think this becomes a stressor only for our husbands, but it's an even bigger problem for *us*. Who has time to prep for an intimate evening when we can't even use the bathroom for fifteen seconds alone in peace? I swear my family has some type of radar for when I step into the bathroom. They don't look for me for hours, but then I walk into any bathroom in our house and, guaranteed, someone's right behind me. How in the world am I supposed to shave or whatever if I can't even tinkle privately? I mean, did you see the list of everything we moms do on the daily? Seriously, we're exhausted by the end of the day, and the last thing we want to do sometimes is have one more person in our personal space. We just want to zone out by ourselves and rest—not think of anything, not answer anyone, not be responsible, just veg and chill. Often at this point in the day, the *last* thing on our minds is making love.

But ladies, hear me out here—being intimate with your husband is more than essential. It's a must. No, seriously, it is the.most.important. thing.you.can.do.for.**yourself**. That ongoing physical connection and exchange of love and care is the lifeblood to a healthy relationship. It's also the lifeblood of your connection to yourself if you're doing it the right way. If you're rolling your eyes and shaking your head thinking, "My marriage is beyond that" or "My husband and I don't need that," believe me—I've been there. If you're thinking this is ridiculous and undermines your beliefs on the foundations of marriage and of being a mom, believe me, I've been there. But as I think back to all of the different points of my relationship with my husband and in my relationship with myself, the happiest periods were the times that the sex was the best and most frequent. It was hot and yummy, and we just couldn't get enough of each other.

In contrast, the hardest times in our relationship and my relationship with myself, even if it wasn't discussed until later, were when we were having passionless, obligatory sex here or there. It's not about the sex, though. It's about my connection with myself. When I'm in a place mentally where I can enjoy sex and my body, I'm in my power. I'm most connected to my life force. I'm turned on to life. I'm in my highest glory. The same is true for my husband. When he's in a place mentally where he can enjoy physical intimacy, he's completely lit up! It starts as being good for each of us individually and then flows over to being good for us and our marriage, our connection, our love.

Life tends to work in phases, I know. There are times it's easier to be and feel sexy, and other times we have to work at it a little more. But take an honest look at the current phase you're in. Consider your relationship's satisfaction level (yours and your husband's) and try to correlate it to the amount (and quality) of sex you're having. "Quality" is the operative word there. If you're having sex often but are only there physically (i.e., running through the grocery list and thinking of what you'll do once this whole thing is over), it's safe to say that it doesn't count. Even though your body may be turned on, you are pinched off mentally, emotionally, and spiritually, and you will not be in your glory. Did you ever orgasm when you were in this place? Highly doubt it. If you catch yourself going through the motions, think about the first few chapters of this book. Are you making yourself a priority? Are you spending time doing things you enjoy? One thing leads to another, so the more you put into yourself keeping your cup full, the less likely you'll be to find yourself in this spot sexually.

Something interesting I've come to realize is that sex can usually be used as a litmus test for an overall marriage condition—you know, the quality of the sex for each partner is directly proportional to the quality of the relationship and contentment of each partner with the other and with themselves. I haven't done an official clinical evaluation or anything on this theory, but, observing my personal experience and the experiences of my friends, I've found this correlation to be true in every case. The couples who are having fulfilling sex have a fulfilling marriage (and are fulfilled with themselves). The couples who aren't in a good place in their marriage are barely having sex, if they're having it at all (and tend not to be tuned in to themselves nor taking time for themselves). This also applies to couples that are having OK sex several times a month—I would guess their marriage is "just OK" as well, with mediocre self-care.

Dare I ask—how is your sex life? Are you satisfied? Do you think your husband is satisfied? Is it AH-mazing? Just OK? Or in danger of extinction? Maybe sex is just another checkbox on your to-do list that you don't get a chance to enjoy as much as your husband because you are too stressed or preoccupied. For a lot of women, it's a challenge because moms don't always feel sexy. It's hard to go from mom-mode to sex kitten in the few minutes of transition after putting the kids to bed, walking down the hallway, and flopping onto the bed in sheer exhaustion. After all, our bodies aren't the same as they were before growing and birthing our babies. Things just look different and sometimes feel different too. You know I love keeping everything in perspective, so let's keep in mind that our husbands are also tired and stressed. What an even better motive to spend some romantic time unwinding together every day! A warm embrace is scientifically proven to reduce stress levels. And, being totally honest, our husbands' bodies have changed post kids too. They may only be able to blame sympathy weight for the dad bod, but seriously, who cares! Love is blind, right? Dim the lights or, better yet, get a black light bulb to swap out for your regular bulb . . . everyone looks more flattering under a black light!

If there are deeper issues about sex that you find for yourself, you're better prepared now to handle them after doing the work on yourself we discussed earlier in this book. Ask yourself the tough questions and be open to what comes up. It's *always* OK to seek help, too, if it all feels too much to handle on your own. This help could be from a coach, therapist, energy healer, or wise friend. Just make sure they encourage you and that you get the results you're looking for. Don't make the novice mistake I made in seeking marriage advice from a friend with a rocky marriage. Shortly after she gave her "great advice," her marriage ended.

The overall point in this section is that you need to step into your power and into your pleasure! Your whole life will radiate brighter because of this decision. You will feel amazing, and your marriage will overflow with love and amazingness as well.

Sexy Goddess Challenge

I'm going to present you with a challenge to get you into this glorious space. This challenge is powerful and will help you regardless of the phase your sex life is in. Ready??

> **It's an "I'll have sex with my husband EVERY DAY for thirty days" challenge, and I nominate YOU!**

Yes, I mean every.damn.day. And yes, I realize you're a busy mom and wife and have a lot going on, and probably the last thing you want to do is this challenge. But hear me out on WHY this is important and what's in it for you.

Think of your last mind-blowing orgasm. I'm talking toes curled, ringing in your ears, seeing stars—wowza! Now fast-forward some. Weren't you a better version of yourself afterward? Did you feel like a freakin' goddess?? And weren't you even more turned on for the next encounter? Hell yeah! When you climax, oxytocin is released, and guess what?? This is the love hormone! No joke! You will not only be a better spouse and mom but also a better person overall by having incredible sex on the regular. You'll feel powerful and like you can do any damn thing you want. I'm pretty sure it's impossible to bitch around about insignificant stuff afterward. Just think. How much will your life improve? Remember how alive (and happy) you felt when you were first falling in love with your partner? How much deeper can that love go now because of all the two of you have lived through together? Being in love is to be in love *on every level*. It's the passion that makes us feel so alive from our connection to ourselves and with another, physically, mentally, emotionally, and spiritually. A lot of people raise an eyebrow here, questioning how in the hell sex can be so transformative. Well, darling, the secret isn't necessarily in the sex itself, but in the preparation of our minds and bodies to get us pumped for the said sex.

Let me explain.

With three night-owl kids, an early school day, and working nonstop on professional and personal stuff during the day, I was/am perpetually exhausted. Prior to doing the thirty-day sex challenge, I wasn't intentional about sex or feeling sexy or pampering myself or even enjoying simple pleasures, like really tasting the ice cream I was treating myself to or soaking up the magnificent sunset. Can you relate to this? I wasn't intentional about my self-care. My days were running me ragged. My sex life was a reflection of this. Without proper planning and intention, by the end of the day, I was spent and had nothing left to give. I knew I wanted to change what I did for my daily routine, and, as fate would have it, I was receiving perfectly aligned info from various sources to piece together the idea for this challenge. At the time, I was intimate with my husband three to four times weekly. I knew that if it was a particularly tough day and we had been intimate the day before, it wasn't a huge deal to let it slide into tomorrow's agenda. There were days I found myself calculating the times I pushed it off to another day, which I then realized was a red flag. In my heart of hearts, sex wasn't something I ever wanted to allow to slip into that perspective of just another task on my to-do list.

The trickiest part of the whole challenge for me wasn't the sex. That was the easiest. The trickiest part was getting my head in the space that it needed to be. It was a daily focus of mine. My perspective had to change. I no longer saw it as a task to check off but as an opportunity to connect and enjoy my partner and myself. I took deliberate steps to prepare my mind and body. I got rid of my ugly underwear and wore the ones I felt good in. I made sure my clothes looked and felt great. I spent time pampering myself, even if it was squeezed into a short chunk of time. I read spicy articles and stories. I checked out new things that my husband and I hadn't tried before or had tried long, long ago. Bottom line—I was *intentional,* and it was fun. The fact that getting in the mood for sex was an everyday thing was *so* helpful to me. It wasn't negotiable. This made a huge difference for me. I didn't give myself space to start that mental conversation when I was tired or uninspired. Instead, I was committed to digging deeper and finding the connection with myself and honoring this challenge.

Maybe you're at a place in your marriage and in your life where you can't imagine having sex every day. I get it. Everyone is on a different path, and there is no one right answer that will work for every person. I encourage you to continue reading, however, and modify the challenge to make sense for where you are. If you haven't had sex in a month or more, you're right; it would be weird to just start having sex every day. How could you explain that one, right? But I would urge you to commit to once a week over the next month with the intention of working up to two or three times a week, to eventually getting to every day. You can still focus on yourself every day and find ways to be more intentional in enjoying yourself. It could be as simple as buying a new mascara or indulging in a decadent dessert—I'm talking really savoring it, noticing how it feels, looks, tastes, and smells. You take it however far you'd like so you feel good and find joy in these activities. You deserve it! Life is meant to be experienced fully and enjoyed!

Maybe you're thinking, "My husband and I have some unresolved issues. I don't feel like having sex until they get resolved." Let me play devil's advocate here. There's something simple about sex and its ability to smooth out some issues. I mean, otherwise, "make-up sex" would have never been coined. Sometimes women don't automatically think of making love to "fix an issue." Please understand, sex itself will not fix unresolved issues, but an ongoing physical connection can pave the way for more connection and intimacy, which promotes a healthier environment to resolve these issues. Usually, we want to talk about the issue, to air all of our grievances and hear how our partner is feeling—and, especially, to tell them how we're reacting to those feelings. But maybe we just need a good dose of the love hormone. I'm not suggesting we do anything against our will, but I *am* talking about getting to a space mentally where we want to be affectionate with our husbands as often as possible. The primary purpose of this challenge is to become empowered with ourselves and take care of our bodies. It's gratifying—in more ways than one!—to decide to fully enjoy yourself and give yourself permission to relax and have pleasurable sex with the man you love. Working on our appreciation lists and making it our job to admire our husbands makes that physical aspect easier and more desirable. We're supposed to be his number-one fan, right? We, myself included, need to step up our games!! Our husbands are so deserving of our love and affection. They need the women of their lives to love them fiercely and show it often. They will be better men because of this—better men for us. And we'll be better women for it.

Like I said, my husband and I were intimate three to four times a week as a rule before this challenge. I would estimate about only half of those times, if that, was I showing up more than just physically for him. I was letting the day-to-day must-dos dominate my mind and didn't take much time for myself consistently. In other words, I was drained and, in trying to do a "good job" for everyone, ended up not doing a good job for anyone, especially myself. Luckily, I came across an article in *Good Housekeeping* by Brittany Gibbons, who wrote about having sex with her husband every day for a year. Mind you, I was sexually active multiple times a week, but something she said stuck out to me in this article. She emphasized the importance of learning to appreciate and enjoy her body. She described how that was one of the biggest rewards of the whole process for her. I knew I was pinched off from myself physically and didn't even give myself a chance to think about "that." I had too much to do, and I was a mom, which was an old belief that wasn't helping me or anyone else that I have since changed. I was intimidated to commit to a whole year of having sex every day but felt that a month was a realistic goal for me. I knew I didn't want to see this as just another to-do on my daily list. My intention for this time was to connect with my husband, improving our intimacy. It was also an important intention for me to enjoy this time, to enjoy my body and do what I needed to do mentally, emotionally, and physically to make the most of that time—to be fully present for myself and also for him. It wasn't about going through the motions. It was about having fun. It wasn't about having an orgasm as much as it was about pleasure. It was about connection. It was about liberation. It was about allowing myself to enjoy and have that time with my husband. So, after finishing the article and doing some research on other ideas related to this, I designed my challenge.

Challenge Rules

* Have sex with your husband every day for thirty days. You may have to initiate it every time, but that's OK. Make sure it happens. Don't wait for the stars to align and both of you to be in the mood or for you both to have smokin' hot bodies—just embrace the moment and your man now. When this was a nonnegotiable part of my day, it was *much* easier to respect this time, and I found myself looking forward to it more than I had in a long time.

* Be sure to make it a point to enjoy yourself fully during each of these encounters. Explore new ideas and new ways of pleasuring yourselves together.

* Show more affection during other parts of the day as well. More hugs, kisses, and words of appreciation for yourself and your spouse.

* Don't mention the challenge to your husband. Of course, you know what will work best in your relationship, but for me, I chose not to say anything about this to my husband at first. I did end up sharing this with him at a later time, but not at the onset. My recommendation here is that you do what you think will work best in your relationship. You can say you're interested in increasing the amount of time you spend together intimately. You can tell him you miss him and the hot sex you shared and would like to get back to more of that. Once you get going into this challenge, you can say the day before was so incredible that you need more. You can tell him that you're really enjoying yourself and seeing him enjoying himself and would like to continue this.

Sexy Tips to Help a Goddess Out

Here are some other tips to help you enjoy this challenge and area of your life much more and improve your marriage as a result:

TIP 1

Change your perspective on sex. It's not something to be checked off the to-do list. It's a fun time that you and your husband can use to express your love for one another. It's your time to fortify your bond and stay connected. Satisfying physical intimacy almost always leads to a great emotional, mental, and spiritual connection as well. You'll have some of your best cuddles and conversations as a result of amazing sex. Please note the key words here: *satisfying* and *amazing*. Don't just assume the position and let him do as he would like. Do what is satisfying to *you*, and you can be sure it will be satisfying for him. I heard it explained once that a man's biggest turn-on is to fully turn on his partner. So, isn't this a win-win? This is your time to get curious and experiment.

A word on orgasms: Keep in mind that about 75 percent of women never reach orgasm from intercourse alone. Seventy-five percent!! Holy moly! That's the majority! This statistic comes from a comprehensive analysis of thirty-three studies over the past eighty years by Elisabeth Lloyd in her book *The Case of the Female Orgasm*. So please don't feel like you are bad at sex for not climaxing during intercourse without other types of stimulation (I'm looking at you, clitoris!). Knowing and accepting this has been a big game changer for me. I no longer feel bad about needing some help to climax, and it's a part of the process for me now, so I'm never looking back!!

TIP 2

Your body is beautiful, flaws and all. You are deserving of affection. You are deserving of love. You are deserving of incredible sex. One of the essential rules of this challenge is that you climax during sex. Why should the guys have all the fun? Our bodies are wonderfully designed and meant to be enjoyed!! Give yourself permission to enjoy this time for yourself with your husband and invest in yourself. Remember that 75 percent of women do not orgasm from vaginal stimulation alone. Be open to exploration and willing to try new things. Adding the use of a vibrator in addition to intercourse will rock your world! Just sayin'!

In conjunction with this challenge, it's extremely beneficial to engage in other sensual things, like bubble baths, self-play and exploration (how can you tell your partner what you like and don't like if you don't know?), dancing, getting massages, buying sexy lingerie, going panty-less . . . the ideas are endless.

TIP 3

Go to bed at the same time as your husband for this challenge. The chance of something taking place once one of you is already asleep is nonexistent. If you're going to the bedroom at the same time, getting ready for bed at the same time, and in the same space at the same time, it will be much easier for you to stick to the challenge. If you and your husband have different schedules and it's not possible to be together due to work or something, plan to be together at a time that works better for the two of you.

TIP 4

Plan sex into your day. Every Single Day. Take a look at your and your husband's schedules and see when the best opportunities would be. Maybe you'll have a window of time when you would usually just catch up on e-mails or watch a show. Instead, schedule in your sexy time. Get creative! It doesn't always have to be in the same place at the same time. Variety is the spice of life. If motherhood has worn you down to the point where you can no longer make plans, I feel you. If you never were a planner because it's just not your style, I can completely relate. Having been a nonplanner *and* a planner, I can say without question that my life goes much smoother and closer to how I would like it to go when I plan it out. That's one of the reasons that the thirty-day challenge is so successful in reconnecting intimately with your spouse—it's planned. You have committed to doin' it and doin' it well.

TIP 5

Research different ideas and read articles on this topic to keep it interesting for yourself and your husband. When you keep the excitement high and the encounters fresh, you'll find it's so much easier to engage. The same way you look for new recipes to try so your family doesn't get sick of the same old dishes over and over again, you can find new ways to spice up your lovemaking so you're both looking forward to it.

TIP 6

Please remember that the same way your joy is unique and personal, so is your marriage. I encourage you to review what you have read so far and take what resonates with you and make it your own. If you aren't comfortable with the "every day for thirty days challenge" because it's been forever since you've had sex, you might want to start at every other day or two times per week. Schedule it in and hold yourself accountable—aka, put it on your calendar and get it done. The idea is that you're making a deliberate effort to engage in more physical connection with your mate. What works for one may not work for another, I completely understand that, but I encourage you to go forward, being open to receiving whatever tips that will help you. There is no "magic checklist" to share that will work with every single marriage, but there are lots of ideas to share that can be adapted and implemented for more love and happiness in your home. The most universal advice I can give that will work across the board is to work on open communication with your spouse and to strive to always be on the same page with one another, especially for the big stuff (for the record: toilet paper rolls facing up or down, while potentially annoying, doesn't count as a big thing). Above all, look for compassion, empathy, nonjudgment, and love every moment you can.

OK, fine, but how do I apply this IRL?

Marriage is one of the most fulfilling and incredible relationships in our lives. Our relationships with our husbands can be fantastic, especially with our inner work being done. Dive into each one of the stressors we've been talking about and question how they apply to your marriage at this time of your life. This isn't a one and done experience, unfortunately. We will frequently need to ask ourselves these and other questions, and we should always be looking for ways to improve our love and our lives. In the whirlwind craziness of motherhood, our sexiness is usually the first thing to get cut out from our day-to-day. The less physical intimacy we have, the less we think we need, but we're just pinching ourselves off from our highest well-being, and everything seems OK until, "all of a sudden," the time catches up to us, and we realize it isn't OK after all. Ask yourself the following questions and reflect on your responses, going as deeply with them as you can:

* What do I love about my husband?
* When was the last time we had an amazing time together?
* What were we doing? How did I feel at that moment?
* When was the best sex of my life?
* What was my life like then?
* What can I do to enjoy my body more?
* What can I do to enjoy myself more with my husband?

Embrace the Magic of Affirmations

* I am perfect just the way I am.
* I am beautiful.
* I love my body and love enjoying all of life's pleasures through all of my senses.
* I feel radiant.

PART 3

All the Jobs Moms Do

CHAPTER 12

Careers In and Out of the Home and Everything in Between

There are two sides to every coin, and while we will discuss stay-at-home moms and working moms and some variations in between in this chapter, I need to stress that no matter what, we are *all* mothers. We all have our successes, and we all have our struggles. They're different in some ways, but when we look deeply, it's easy to notice that the main areas are the same for all moms. I would encourage you to read each section of this chapter even if you aren't in the particular situation it discusses. I remember being a working mom and feeling envious of the stay-at-home moms based on my fantasy of what that must be like. Then I became a stay-at-home mom and confronted the common stressors firsthand that weren't a part of that original fantasy at all. There are overlapping stressors that are mentioned in different sections in this chapter. Each section in this chapter highlights important points that all moms can relate to and need to hear regardless of how they spend their days.

During my motherhood journey, I have been all of these. Moms often change careers or roles as the demands of the family change. Throughout your journey, you may find yourself in any combination of these careers as well. Please revisit this chapter when that happens. When all is said and done, it's how we support one another regardless of the path we each choose that matters the most. We are doing amazing work both inside and outside the home, and everything in between.

Stay-at-Home Moms

There are countless blessings from this full-time job! We can all recite the quotes that say the most precious jewels ever to be around your neck will be the arms of your children and how wonderful it is to have the opportunity to be present for so much of your child's life. We love our children and can't imagine doing anything else. But . . . the days are long. No, we aren't just sipping our lattes while the kiddos joyously play at the park in perfect harmony with the other kids all day, every day. No, we aren't just lounging around and have a bonus break during nap time. I'll be the first to tell you that the days are LOOOOONG! Everyone knows the years are short, but man oh man! Are those days long!! There's a lot of crying and talking and whining and convincing and compromising and creating. There's a lot of planning and cheering. And, always, there's a lot of love.

In the position of SAHM, we're required to be self-taught, quick thinkers with the patience of Job. We need to be visionaries. We're raising someone's future wife or husband! We're raising someone's best friend. If we lose sight of this bigger picture, it's easy to get swept up in the idea that what we're doing in our mundane, day-to-day routine doesn't matter. We aren't doing anything important. We are on duty every day of the year and on call every night, and we're the answer to many, many of our child's problems. If we don't keep our "bigger picture" on our radar, we run the risk of forgetting just how important our role is. If nothing else, we're setting the example for our children. We're modeling for them the type of person they should be. Ahhh! That can be scary! But make sure you're setting your best example as often as you can, because even when we think the kids are focused on something else, they're also tuned in to their mama. Don't believe me? Drop one f-bomb under your breath around your toddler who's playing in the next room. We've all been there. No judgments.

But even though we moms are the center of our family's universe, one of the biggest stressors as a stay-at-home mom can be feeling like we aren't making a difference. Sometimes we need to put in the work first before we can see what is good and what's not. I had my first two children back-to-back, only fourteen months apart. It wasn't until the second was almost two years old that I realized how exhausting it all had been for me up to that point. I was drained in every possible way.

It also took about that long to realize something else. I was at the playground with a moms' group I had joined, and that lovely second born of mine was playing and enjoying himself when one of the other toddlers got hurt. The injury was nothing serious, but the little boy had bumped his knee and was crying for his mom. My son was right next to his friend when he got hurt and offered a hug to help him feel better. When the other mom had reached her son, I picked up mine, hugged him, and acknowledged his sweet gesture, and then he went on playing as per usual. The other mom also noticed the kindness, and, after her son was calm, came and thanked me for what my son had done. You might have thought that I won a major award the way her comment made my month!! She said, "You can always tell a loving parent by a loving child." This woman couldn't have said anything nicer to me if she wanted to. It was the exact message I needed.

I had spent the previous two years doing my best but constantly wondering if it was "right" or if it was enough. I would question my talent as a mother and doubt myself on an almost-constant basis. The simple declaration of another mom at the playground gave me strength I could draw from on the harder days of raising two toddlers. I can still feel the warm happiness that washed over me as I stood on the mulch that day. I had been putting in the work every day for a couple of years before seeing one of the first results of my labor. I finally had some validation that it was working.

The sidebar to this story is to remind us of the importance of seeing something nice and saying something. That day was the first and only time in my life that I saw that mom. She had no idea what I was going through, what I was like with my kids, or who I was. But she noticed something nice about someone and shared it with them. I doubt she even remembers that exchange, but I can't begin to describe how important that comment was to me. You never know how your kindness will impact another. If you see anything you admire in someone else, please tell them—especially if she's a mom.

130 All the Jobs Moms Do

There are so many trivial tasks in motherhood and so many mundane moments that we begin to question the importance of what we do. Of course we "make a difference," because if we didn't clean up, we know the house would be a wreck. Yes, that's making a difference, but is it a meaningful difference? It's easy to get caught up in the humdrum, day-to-day SAHM life and begin to doubt the importance of what we do. If we let it continue, we can begin to doubt our importance as well. There are so many average moments in a family's daily routine. What's glamorous about brushing your toddler's teeth or wiping kids' butts? There's no spotlight and round of applause for preparing breakfast for your child or packing his lunch with healthy choices. No one posts photos of explaining fraction homework to a third grader or reading *Are You My Mother?* one more time before bed. I have yet to see widespread posts of people loading their dishwasher or putting leftovers in a fridge that needs to be cleared out rather than stuffed with more food. But I challenge you to question whether these moments are less important to your children and your family just because they're average and mundane.

Our culture has become obsessed with oversharing on social media. While the online world can provide tons of brilliant insights, life hacks, and connections, it can also mislead us. We can be pulled into the illusion that our houses always need to be pristine, our families always need to be happy, and our lives always need to be fun. No one posts anything of the shit show of a morning they had trying to get their kids up and off to school or the embarrassing disaster of their home after some family time spent there. The glamorous, amazing, everything-is-always perfect Instagram life IS NOT REAL. Messes are normal. Things being out of place and dirty dishes piled on the counter and clothes scattered around in your home are normal. Having a disagreement with your partner is normal. Recognizing what you need to work on is normal. Getting frustrated with your kids is normal. Being tired is normal. Not wanting to do your chores is normal. Doing your best and wondering if it is enough is normal. NORMAL is normal. Normal is not bad. It is *impossible* to have a perfect, social-media-ready life 24/7.

Of course, there are moments that are glamorous. And sweetheart, soak those bad boys up when they come!! And in the moments that aren't glamorous, please recognize that they aren't bad—you aren't doing anything wrong. They're still opportunities to love and moments that you and your kids have together. As I look back on my childhood, some of the most "normal" memories are the most special ones. Just because you aren't having a big-deal moment, that doesn't make it less important. There's still a chance to show your love to your kids and to let your example lead the way.

The same way it's hard to see our tremendous contribution in the normalcy of life, it's also hard to see our contribution when we have other expectations of ourselves (or others have them of us). You know, adulting expectations, like making money. We correlate success with how much money we make, and as a stay-at-home mom, that's often zero. But don't fall into the trap of "I'm just staying at home with the kids, and because I'm not doing more to help financially, I'm failing my family." I said these words at one point. I had started working as soon as I was legally old enough. I loved having my own money and picking and choosing what I was going to do with it. When I was a stay-at-home mom, I had some issues with not working and not having "my own" money. OK, don't judge me. Our limiting beliefs usually don't make much sense. Of course, I fully understood the concept of marriage and of two becoming one, including finances. I understood that I was making enormous contributions to my family's lives in other ways, but it always irked me that financially I wasn't contributing. I even put a spin on it by trying to save as much money as possible, and that was my financial contribution. The ironic part of this is that when we were first married, I worked while my husband didn't for a season and again when he opened up his first company.

During these two phases, I was the sole breadwinner. I was working and never saw that money as "my money" but always as our money. I'm not sure why, when the tables were turned, I thought I was in a different relationship. My husband was always supportive and never acted as though he thought our money was really "his money." He made it a point to express his gratitude for what I was doing in our home and with our children, but most times, that fell on deaf ears. This was an issue for me because of old beliefs I had from the past. It was stuff that I had to work through. I believed that I wasn't doing enough without making a financial contribution. I thought my earnings directly reflected my success and my worth. If I wasn't contributing financially, I was a burden to my family. Who cared that I was doing other stuff that could never be measured with a bank account?! I had taken such pride in my work and the money that came from it. It became part of my identity, and when I didn't have that anymore, I forfeited part of my self-worth with it. These beliefs were holding me back from freedom and needed to be let go. Sounds pretty easy, huh? Just let go to be free. Well, hate to burst any bubbles, but letting go isn't always as easy as "just letting go." It can be scary to release a belief, even when you have evidence that it's not doing you any good. We're often afraid of what we don't know, even when there's a good chance of it being better than what we currently have.

But perhaps something that feels worse than not contributing is feeling completely alone. For the stay-at-home mom, isolation is no stranger. It's a lot of work to talk to kids all day with little to no adult interaction. Even when you do get the chance to meet up with a friend at a playdate, there's no guarantee you two will have a chance to truly connect. It will depend on how the kids are behaving and who skipped a nap that day. I once met up with a dear friend, and we barely talked due to sheer exhaustion. Our kids were thrilled to be together and happily played, but there was minimal conversation between the moms who were plain worn out on that hot summer day.

Just knowing that feeling isolated at times in motherhood is a normal feeling takes a lot of the pressure off. If you're in a phase where you feel like you don't have a lot of people who can understand your life, and you can't feel connected to anyone on a deep enough level, please know that *this is normal*, and all moms at one point or another may go through this. Feelings like this can increase during major life changes, like moving or having a baby. There's so much happening during any given day that we can't easily share with another. It would take too long to explain, and ain't nobody got time for that. So we keep it to ourselves and feel alone.

Knowing that other women are going through similar situations takes a lot of the loneliness out of the equation. Keeping the bigger perspective in mind as well and seeing this as only a phase will also help. When you're in the midst of this, when one day seems to be as long as one week because of all of the mental chatter, physical demands, and stress, we can't always see the light at the end of the tunnel. But just because we can't see it doesn't mean that it's not there. We will get there eventually. Everything is a phase, especially in parenting, and all phases pass. Until they do, we just gotta keep breathing and doing our best for ourselves and our loved ones.

Time for yourself, although seemingly the opposite of what you're looking for, can be an important game changer. If you're able to relax and let go and be with yourself in a quiet moment, you can feel the peace and serenity increase within and around you. If you happen to be in a phase of feeling particularly isolated, make it a point to schedule time during the week to interact with those you love. This could be catching up with a friend while your kids nap or while you do laundry or arranging a lunch date with your husband while the kids are in school to have a meal together with some uninterrupted conversation. You could venture out and join a new group or visit family more often. You'll know the ideas that will make the most sense for you. When you find the right ones, schedule them in and make it a point to follow through on those plans. Your future self will thank you!

There were lots of times as a SAHM when I would run into a friend while out and about, and they would ask the very typical question, "So, what have you been up to?" I would have a total brain fart and never really know how to answer. I was a stay-at-home mom. I was going nonstop all day. I was up to a lot of stuff, but there was nothing really "interesting" to report. There were lots of times I felt isolated by this. I was in this self-contained bubble that only my closest people got to witness. It was tricky to put a positive spin on that for my acquaintances, especially ones who were in a different situation from me. A lot of times, I didn't have much to contribute to the conversation, and it was challenging not to let that affect me emotionally. I wasn't as up-to-date on the things that I used to be, but I could talk about *Dora the Explorer* or which parks had the best slides and working bathrooms. One of the best things I did to support myself during this time was to find a moms' club in my area. It's so refreshing to be with other women who are in the same phase as you. They get the craziness. They'll be there to swap ideas and tricks of the trade. They'll listen to your stories and take an interest in your kids. They'll support you, even if only for that phase of your life.

Another major stressor for SAHMs is the minimal to no downtime. This is particularly true of moms with younger children. When you're a mom, you're the most needed person in your child's life. Sure, dads are important too, as are other loved ones, but when push comes to shove, which happens to be every three minutes for a toddler, the kids need their mama. While it's great to be this sanctuary for our little cherubs, this safe place, this refuge, it's freaking exhausting. The sheer frustration that comes from trying to get a simple task done with someone hanging on you, interrupting you, poking you, telling you they love you (I mean, at this point you feel like an ass for even thinking about getting mad), asking what seems to be 4,356,281 questions while coughing or sneezing on you is enough to make most people want to cry. Self-care and taking time for yourself is critical. I remember the first few occasions I took time for myself when my boys were little. I was so depleted that I would get angry when my time was up. I get hints of this nowadays when I'm not taking the necessary time for myself. I try to squeeze something in, and time runs short, and I find myself gasping, "Gah! Already?!" So please know that if you take some time for yourself and, when it's over, you feel frustrated, angry, or sad, these are indicators that you need more time for yourself on a more consistent basis. It's a sign you're burned out and need to fill up that cup. No problem; just make a plan to make yourself a priority again. When I'm not depleted and I have some time for myself, I'm able to return to the fray feeling happy. Our emotions are always guiding us if we are aware of them. The stay-at-home mom may appear to be cool, calm, and collected from the outside, although at times it's pure fake-it-to-make-it survival. Through that, though, she naturally evolves into this woman who can multitask and get things done while simultaneously solving big issues with her kids. It's no small feat to prepare an entire dinner with a baby nearby playing—or a toddler for that matter, let alone with said toddler clinging to your leg while you cook. Kids require nonstop attention, feedback, and love. They're amazing and wonderful and deserve all of our best and more, but man oh man, when you're in the thick of your day, and you're just about out of patience, it's hard to remember that. "Up, please!" isn't always as fun the 157th time that day. We moms get tired of being touched and being the problem solvers. We get tired from making all of the decisions. Being on call all day every day catches up to us *fast*. We can quickly become that mom who angrily snaps at her kids, barking out commands: "Stop!" or "Sit down!" or "No!" Then, once we've had a chance to breathe, we go into our children's rooms and watch them sleep and feel like a bad mom for those snaps. We guilt ourselves and promise to try harder the next day and start out with the best of intentions, but as the day wears on, we become less and less patient and more and more tired.

This less-patient and more-tired mom version of me was never more apparent than when my children stopped napping. Naptime, especially for SAHMs, is GOLDEN. Mama *needs* her kids to nap, so when my kids each stopped napping at only a year-and-a-half old, I was a nutcase. It wasn't for my lack of trying; they just didn't need that nap. If they had it, they would be up until all hours of the night, which was even worse than not napping. So you know what I had to do? I had to find another time during my day that I was doing something for myself. I needed to find time for me in between the craziness of running around after two toddlers. Driving became one of those times for me. We would go out for the morning and the kids would play their hearts out. On the way back, even if they didn't officially sleep, they were zoning out in their own toddler dimension, and that meant I had a break for a bit. If the stars aligned and the kids would fall asleep, I wouldn't dare try to move them. I hung out in the car with them, doing my own things, like talking to a friend or reading a book.

I also got good at planning my days with fun activities and everything to make it easier for myself later on. Once the kids had that special time with me, and I had a chance to connect with each of them individually, they were less needy and more open to playing by themselves. The days that my planning didn't play out and I was "busy" doing mom stuff were the toughest days—always! The kids needed my love and attention first. Once they had that, they were more OK with letting me take time to work on my projects or even take a trip to the bathroom alone. I'm telling you, it's the small things in life!

I urge all of the stay-at-home moms to question your day-to-day routines and see how you can incorporate more "special time" with your children. Maybe it's once in the morning and again in the afternoon for them to feel satisfied. Try it and see what seems to work best. To clarify, when I say "special time," I'm referring to a time that you and your child have together, doing an activity of their choice and/or yours with little or no other distractions. So this isn't a time that I'm on my phone, watching a show, cooking a meal, or anything else. I'm with my child in the moment. If you don't know what to do, the best idea is to ask your child what he or she would like to do. Make sure to have a good attitude about it—if you're bored during the activity, don't feel bad. Bring it up a level for yourself and take notice of your child. Admire his eyelashes, or how her eyes squint when she's trying to come up with a name for her toy. Take note of the little details: what do you see, hear, smell, taste, and feel? You can make mental notes of this, but you might want to jot some of these things down later in the day because the time goes by so fast, and you probably won't remember all of those amazing details. You'll be so thankful to have a memory of them later on.

I don't mean to imply that we'll miss every part of this phase. I'm positive I won't miss anyone throwing up in the middle of the night—or at any time, for that matter—or the ridiculous temper tantrums or sassy back talk when I make a simple request or say no to something, but I know there are plenty of sweet moments I will terribly miss when they don't happen anymore. Those are the moments that I want to cherish and remember forever.

I had my first real taste of this bittersweet truth last summer. When my boys were preschoolers, we would buy a family season pass to Sesame Place each year. It's a theme park close to our house and based on the show *Sesame Street*, which is ideal for younger kids. The boys and

I would pick a weekday to go once a week during the summer and enjoy the rides, play in the water, and dance as we watched the street party parade. I remember I would put in a Sesame Street CD and blast the theme song "Sunny Days" as we pulled into the parking lot each time. The windows were down, warm air blew my boys' sweet brown hair back, and enormous smiles were on their faces as we all sang at the top of our lungs. I knew in those moments that I would miss them in the future, but I only found out how much this past summer.

We had friends visiting from Brazil with their three-year-old daughter, and one of the obvious places to take them was to Sesame Place. Our guests were excited by this idea, but the boys weren't. By that point, they were twelve and eleven and said they didn't want to go. My four-year-old daughter was on board, though, so we were good to go. I didn't think much of the boys saying they didn't want to go at first, because it's not a place geared to their age nor interests. I wasn't surprised they weren't interested in going. I actually expected them to say they didn't want to go, but it wasn't until we were pulling into the parking lot that it hit me. The song wasn't playing, the windows weren't down, and my little boys weren't with me. Realizing this, I looked at my daughter and tried to soak up all of her magic in that moment, knowing how quickly it would grow into something else equally lovely yet extremely different.

In the park, it was fun to see my daughter experience those rides and attractions the same way the boys had several years earlier, but there was a heavy, bittersweet feeling in my heart. I knew how precious those moments were as I was living them. I'm proud to say that I fully enjoyed the time with my boys on our Sesame Place days and many other occasions, as well. But in that moment, I realized that phase with them was completely over. I only had those heartwarming memories now. It honestly doesn't seem like that much time has gone by. I feel like I was there only a couple of summers ago. That day in the theme park with my friends from Brazil, and in the weeks following, I put extra emphasis on being present and appreciating the phases my kids are in now. I'm so glad that I did this from when they were little, and I am extraordinarily blessed to have so many special memories with them.

It wasn't all sunshine and puppies, though. The kids and I had our share of rough days. I wasn't always as patient as I would have liked to be, nor did I have some of the powerful tools I have today to use to be a better mom. I used to be the mom who would get frustrated and let that frustration carry over into other parts of the day, even if the initial frustration had passed. So if one of my boys had a meltdown at a playdate and we had to leave early, I would carry that frustration later into that day. Even if the kids did something cute or funny or lovely, I wouldn't acknowledge it because I was still irritated from earlier. But the same way we can choose what wave we ride with our husbands, we can always choose what wave we ride with our kids.

I know I should have seen my children with more compassion at times and understood that they were only toddlers or kids. I'm proud of the times that I did. I'm proud of the times I was able to move on quickly from the irritation I felt. I'm proud of those examples that I was showing them. For everything else, I know I was doing the best I could with what I knew at that time. I choose to see the love in the situation and learn from the experience.

Motherhood, especially SAHM-dom, can be an all-consuming experience. We need to make sure to make time for ourselves, to be gentle with ourselves when we don't, and to take it all with a grain of salt. We will have good days and will have shitty days. Sometimes our kids will cooperate and other times they won't—like, not even a little bit. Please believe me when I tell you that it's OK—all of it.

The best advice I can give you is that this stay-at-home-mom thing is just a phase. The same way that pregnancy came and went, the stay-at-home mom phase will pass as well. Eventually, our kids go to school or graduate and go off on their own. Remember this, especially on the tough days. Enjoy the crazy. Enjoy the active, nonstop day-to-day, full of life. Enjoy your kids. They are only little once. You only have that time with them once. It's amazing that you have this opportunity to spend this time with the little people who mean the world to you. It can be incredibly difficult, but it can also be extremely fun and rewarding. The years that I stayed with my kids were some of the BEST years of my life. I'm the first to say that there were days that I just wanted to cry and others that I wanted to scream, but looking back now, I cherish the extra time I had with my sons and daughter and wouldn't trade it for anything.

Working Moms

This section is dedicated to the mom who works a job of forty or more hours per week, even if they are technically "part-time." I mean, *all moms* are working moms, am I right? But for the sake of this section, I'm focusing on the mamas at their J-O-B, their career. The biggest stressor for working moms is time. Factoring in a full-time job with the already nonstop, full-time job of motherhood can put a tremendous amount of stress on us moms! Planning becomes a necessary saving grace, but with that need for tight schedules comes the sergeant attitude. We need to set times and have everyone in our family follow those times so we can do allllllll that we need to do in the short amount of time we have to do it. It becomes difficult to enjoy the ride when there is so much to manage. We can feel like we need to be on guard at all times, ready to make the next command so we can do it all or at least make sure it all gets done somehow or another. We are always just one sick child away from mass chaos in our perfectly calculated plans.

But if we aren't careful, we can stifle our creativity, as well as our child's, with this serious approach. It's essential to be mindful of how much we are or aren't enjoying our day-to-day life. Does it make sense to force yourself and your family to do things that no one really wants to for the sake of checking it off a to-do list? I'm not saying you shouldn't get your kids to bathe if they don't want to, but I'm thinking more along the lines of activities, commitments, etc. Your children do need enriching activities, yes. But more importantly, they need a strong connection with their parents. Can you connect with your child on the way to soccer? Sure! I'm only encouraging you to examine your commitments and your children's commitments and be very protective of your time together, especially as a working mom. You only have a certain amount of time each evening and weekend with your family. That time is sacred. So, yes, it's important to clean and organize the house, attend birthday parties, and do the usual stuff that parents and kids are supposed to do, but it's essential you have moments within that sacred time for only you and your child—a time to connect and bond with one another. It's OK to say no to obligations and activities in order to tend to your relationship with your child. The magic here is definitely in the *quality* of the time you both spend together. Imagine how incredible of a feeling to know that your parents canceled or rearranged plans to be with you! That's a pretty special feeling. Doing this will help us be less drill sergeant and more enjoyable to be around and easier to connect with. Our stress levels will reduce, and everyone will benefit. When we're clear about our top priorities and schedule them in first, we're setting loving boundaries to prepare ourselves for success.

When we don't plan around our top priorities, we tend to handle life in a responsive manner to all things urgent, setting ourselves up for unnecessary stress. This major stressor for working moms is widely known as "mom guilt." Of course, this is not exclusive to working moms, but it can be a pretty heavy weight on any working mom's shoulders. You know, the second-guessing of whether we're doing the right thing when we drop off our precious tots to daycare or a sitter or turning away an excited child because we have work to do, either for our jobs or for our family; after all, someone has to make dinner and do the laundry. We can often be found saying, "OK, but first let me just . . ." (fill in the blank: squeeze in another chore or e-mail or phone call or text). We will go into more detail on mom guilt in the next chapter. Moms are big-time multitaskers. We have so much to do in such little time. Multitasking is grand but, at the same time, can be a real time sucker. I've found that when I'm 100 percent engaged with my kids and put everything else on hold, the "everything else" still gets done when needed. When I multitask and try to get two or more things done at once, I've found that it usually blows up in my face on at least one side.

Mama, let's be deliberate with our time. I heard of the concept of block scheduling from Jordan Page of *Fun Cheap or Free*. I started listening to her advice, and it didn't sound too bad. She totally sold me when she said she had five kids with the sixth on the way. I thought, "OK, if this works for a mom of six, I will give this a try!" So I took her tips on block scheduling, which include identifying blocks in which I am electronic-free (i.e., no phone or laptop), and put together my own schedule with chunks of time instead of going hour by hour. Wow! I was amazed to see the difference when I'm not multitasking.

When my kids are home, I'm with them. I'm focused on them. I'm enjoying that time. When I'm at work, I'm focused on work. I've given myself freedom by chunking my day into blocks and focusing on specific things during specific times. I also give a better version of myself to each block as opposed to trying to spin all of my plates at once. After implementing this system, I don't feel guilty anymore about not spending enough time with my kids or about not getting enough done. Everything has its time and gets taken care of. While it may seem counterproductive, it actually has helped me to get so much more done in my day without pulling my hair out at failed attempts of doing too many things simultaneously, and none of them very well. The same way we need to protect our time and how we spend it as moms, we also need to be very deliberate with it. It's easier to maintain when everything has a place, even our schedules.

Another common working-mom problem that has a seemingly counterproductive solution is little to no time for self-care. We know we need to take care of ourselves first before we can effectively take care of others. We know what we need to do to feel recharged and to find our Zen. We even know that we need to schedule that time for ourselves. However, busy moms often make the mistake of cutting "their time" out of the schedule first.

Does this example of a day in the life of a working mom sound familiar?

> I try to wake up a little before my family to have time to myself but end up snoozing my alarm. I wake up at the last minute and rush to get myself and the kids up, ready, and out the door. I pack lunches, make sure everyone has what they need for their day, walk the kids to the bus stop or drop them off to school, and slide into work without a minute to spare, wondering if I brushed my teeth or remembered to start the crockpot for dinner.

At work, I help coworkers and clients to make sure they're all taken care of. People come to me with questions, and I help them with whatever they need. I grab a quick lunch and eat at my desk to finish a project with an upcoming deadline. I quickly text my husband to check in on his day and tell him I love him. I think of the kids and hope they're all having good days. I put two more things on the grocery list that I just remembered and get back to my work for the afternoon.

I leave the second my workday ends and am off to pick up my kids. On the way home, I stop at the grocery store to pick up aforesaid items and squeal into the driveway in time to meet my husband. After unloading the car, backpacks, groceries, and lunch boxes and getting things situated to repack many of these items, I make the rest of dinner and am relieved that I did remember to turn on the crockpot! I clear the table (because it also serves as a catch-all-the-crap shelf), and then I call in the troops. Everyone's hungry and needs something. I get drinks, refill plates, and, after a whirlwind of forks clattering and food disappearing (from everyone's plates except mine because who has time to eat?), dinner is over. I clean the dishes, store leftovers, and try to work with kids on their homework, reviewing math facts and spelling words, all while picking up out-of-place items and returning them to their designated spots on my way from place to place in this routine.

Once things are wrapped up, I corral everyone upstairs for bath time. I make sure teeth are brushed, clothes are laid out for the next day, and kids are hugged, kissed, and tucked in. I listen to the happenings of the day and give feedback on whatever topics come up. I try to remember to send a specific item tomorrow for a show-and-tell or that the following Tuesday is pajama day for someone. I read to the kids and turn out the lights. I then head downstairs to finish the chores and, hopefully, have some time to flop down on the sofa and decompress a bit before it's time for me to head to bed. My husband and I talk some and then we make the final preparations for the next day and head to tuck ourselves in. I'd like to read some while he's showering or stretch or make a gratitude list, but I end up on my phone, scrolling through my feed, too exhausted to do much of anything else. I take a deep breath and try to exhale the weight of the day. I do the math of how much sleep I'll get if I fall asleep in twenty minutes and wonder if that will be enough to get me through tomorrow. I turn out the lights, ready—or not—to repeat all of this the next day.

Maybe this sounds too familiar, or maybe you need to change some of the details, but either way, notice that in this example, there wasn't one thing this mom did for herself. She was up and giving, giving, giving the whole day. That's natural for moms. I know that's our job, but you can only give and give and give for so long before you become depleted unless you're refueling yourself. Sleep is important, and, in the example, the mom hoped the sleep would be enough, but often it isn't. What about diet and exercise? In this example, there was no indication of a heavy focus on diet and/or exercise. It's an important piece of the puzzle, though. It's easier to feel good when we're healthy and well.

Additionally, there wasn't anything this mom did that was specifically for her, or because she wanted to, or for fun. Of course, she enjoyed the time with her kids and had fun with them. No question that she enjoyed her conversation with her husband. He's her favorite person to talk to, after all. But there wasn't something specific that she did for herself.

This will be different for each of us, but always include something that brings you joy in your day. Something just for you. It could be as simple as a five-minute break to have a cup of tea and gaze out the window at the beautiful sky or to go on a ten-minute walk in a park. It could be a twenty-minute call to a girlfriend or relative to catch up and laugh together. It could be a lunch date with your husband or even with yourself. You could schedule an art class or something new to try out. Explore life and have fun! We're looking for quality here—stuff that simply lights you up.

My favorite way to view success in my life isn't to gauge it by possessions, money, or accomplishments, but to measure it by the amount of joy I feel. I want to be a successful mom for my children. I want to be joyful. I want to have fun. I want to share joy with my family and have millions of happy moments. I want to be the most successful person I know in this measure of success, feeling absolutely joyful every day, even on the not-so-good ones. I know taking time for myself in different ways throughout the day, week, month, and year will provide me with ongoing joy. I know that even though I'm busy, it's imperative that I make time for myself.

If we don't make this our main priority, life has a way of creeping in, and, ever so slowly, we become worn down to the point of little joy. And that causes us to become the edgy mom, the one who is past the point of reason. There's no quick pep talk to bring us back to joy, no positive spin we can put on it. We're in a funk, one that is rooted in not bringing joy into our day-to-day experience. I'm most edgy and will bite someone's freakin' head off the quickest—usually someone I love most—when I have an issue with myself, or when I haven't been giving myself enough me time. It's usually when there isn't time to waste, and I need to get stuff done. It's crunch time—no time for self-care and doing what feels good. Gotta roll my sleeves up and persevere no.matter.what. Well, that never lasts for long, because when I try to make it happen, I wind up getting sick or hitting some other type of wall. My body stands up to this craziness and revolts in its own way, forcing me to slow down and provide time to reconnect with myself.

We need to carve out space daily for ourselves to be us and do what we enjoy. We need that consistent connection with ourselves to stay balanced and healthy and to keep the edginess away. It may seem counterintuitive to take time for yourself—possibly even extra time for yourself—when you're beyond busy, but it's one of the biggest life changers I've encountered to date. The crazier my schedule is, or the fuller my to-do list becomes, the more important it is for me to take time for myself. A half hour here or there during the day becomes a reviving solitude that's crucial to my well-being.

Careers In and Out of the Home and Everything in Between   145

We shouldn't feel guilty or like we're mismanaging our time. We need to be good. We need to feel good. We need to take care of ourselves so we can better care for our families.

If you're a working mom, you might feel that you're trapped in between the two worlds of work and home with little connection to one or the other. It's so easy to get into the mindset of produce, produce, produce that it becomes nearly impossible to be 100 percent present in either area. When you're at work, you're thinking about home life. When you're with the family, you're thinking about work. There will always be activities, teachable moments, deadlines, and expectations. It's imperative to make a conscious effort to be fully present wherever you are. Applying this in my own life has helped me to accomplish so much more than ever before. I have been able to produce more in each area in less time when I'm solely focused on that given area for that chunk of time. For me, this means being as drastic as keeping my phone away from myself during a certain block of time, depending on the activity.

If I'm with my kids, I want to be *with* my kids, engaging in conversation and play, not doing the half-listening "mmhmm, mmhmm " response thing. If I'm working on a project for work, I want to be there 100 percent. Have you ever tried to write an important e-mail with your children around? What could normally take five minutes tops becomes a forty-five-minute event. After stubbornly going through this several times, I've learned it's better first to address my child fully and then send the e-mail with undivided attention at a later time. My energy isn't split, and I'm way more productive. I'm also less stressed and cranky as a result.

This suspension between the two worlds can be very isolating. As a working mom, you also tend to have less time to catch up with friends and socialize, even at the office. Fewer fun times mean a broader isolated feeling. It's a good idea to schedule lunch with friends as often as you can, and, of course, coworkers can count. On the days that it's too crazy to do lunch, you can make a call to catch up with a friend or loved one during your commute. If you aren't driving, exting is always a quick option to stay in touch, so if you're waiting for a meeting to start and have a sec, just say hi. You could even do a quick search and see what cool events are

146 All the Jobs Moms Do

going on near you this weekend and invite a friend or two to go with. It takes some effort, but it is well worth it.

Working moms can feel like they're being pulled in all directions. We need to make sure we're responsible and get creative with how we spend our time. Being clear on what's most important is essential in doing this. We need to be flexible when things don't work out according to our plans and always look for ways to feel good. We need to honor our careers and our livelihoods, the same as we honor our families. We can do it, be it, and have it all as long as we believe that we can. If that feels shaky in any way, check back to chapter 5, where we talked about rewriting our beliefs. What do you want to believe is possible for you? Otherwise, keep up the fantastic job with affirmations and enjoying your career, your family, and your badass self.

Hybrid Moms

With the convenience of technology, there's a new opportunity for careers, which I call the hybrid model. You can work from anywhere with an Internet connection. You have flexible hours, and you get the best (and worst) of both the stay-at-home-mom and working-mom worlds. You'll (generally) be able to attend all of the school shows and activities, and you'll still be able to have meetings, make a living, and, hopefully, have some time to focus on yourself in there as well. Oftentimes, the hybrid mom is self-employed. Like the SAHM, the hybrid mom has the time and flexibility to perform many of the ongoing chores, like laundry, dishes, and dinner, while she works. She can spend time with her kids, take them to extracurricular activities, run errands, and the like. Similar to the working mom, she has responsibilities outside of the home. She has deadlines to meet, and people who are counting on her. She can let her talents shine as she helps her clients.

What's different for the hybrid mom is that she doesn't have well-defined blocks of time and has too many expectations coming from too many sides at any given time. For example, my clients don't want to hear that I couldn't get back to them sooner because I was chaperoning my son's field trip or that I can't meet during a certain time because of dance

Careers In and Out of the Home and Everything in Between   147

lessons. They're working with the professional version of me and mean business. Their expectation isn't always a match for my reality for this phase of my life. My family, on the other hand, counts on me and expects me to be there for them when they need me. So when one of my kids is sick and needs to stay home from school, my husband doesn't take off and stay home from the office so I can work. I scrap that day and try my best to fit in as much as I can in any window of time that I have that day. My hybrid-mom friend expressed it best when she said, "It's either a good mom day or a good workday."

Hybrid moms feel like they are being pulled in all directions like working moms; however, they feel this at all times because there isn't a clear divide between work and home. They feel like they have to produce as though they work full-time and take care of the family and home like they are a stay-at-home mom. It's an impossible dilemma, actually. It can be frustrating to have time limits on what you can do at home or at work in this type of career, but remember that this is only for a phase of time. Everything will pass. It'll get more manageable, and you'll have more time to focus on your endeavors. In the meantime, focus on what's most important and make some ruthless decisions accordingly. Mom guilt is a huge pain point for these hybrid-career moms. There's always that question in the back of your mind: "Did I do enough today?" for both family and work.

OK, fine, but how do I apply this IRL?

Mama, regardless of what you do, know that you're doing your best, and your kids are lucky to have you in their lives. So if you work at home, outside of the home, full-time, or part-time, or if you're a SAHM, it's totally awesome. All of it. I encourage you to embrace the beautiful chaos of the phase you're in right now and find the love and beauty. Sometimes that looks like sacrifice, sometimes that looks like "good enough," even when you think you could/should do better, and other times that looks like total adoration and joy. If you're a stay-at-home mom, working mom, or any variation of hybrid mom, please know that you deserve to be one of your top priorities. Taking good care of yourself and bringing more joy to your days will help you excel in any and all of these roles. You got this, mama!

Embrace the Magic of Affirmations

* I am a good mom.
* I am lucky to have my kids, and they are lucky to have me.
* I am grateful for the time I spend with my kids each day.
* I take care of myself to better take care of my family.

Stay-at-Home Mom Phase

* I am more than "just" a mom.
* My job as a mom can never be measured by a bank account.
* I am making enormous contributions to my children even when I can't see it.

Working Mom Phase

* When at work, I give my full attention and excel.
* When at home, I give my full attention and enjoy.
* I am making huge contributions to my family in every way.

Hybrid Mom Phase

* I adapt with ease for the tasks at hand.
* I am amazed at all that I can accomplish in a day at home and work.
* I enjoy what I do as a mom and as a professional and am greatly compensated for it.

CHAPTER 13

More Than "Just" a Mom

In this chapter, we'll discuss kids and everything else that we haven't yet discussed. "Wait," I hear you saying, "kids lumped in with everything else? That's messed up!" While motherhood is thought to be about the kids, it's really just as much about us as mothers. When our child was born so was our motherhood. We are women, and we are proud of that, or at least we would like to be, but we are more than that. Parenting could possibly be the MOST important thing you will ever, ever do in your whole life. But you are more than just a mom. Being a mom is merely one part of who you are. And the best thing you can do as a mother, or human being, for that matter, is to stay balanced and work on yourself. To be the best version of yourself, you need to take a look at yourself as a whole.

It's in your wholeness that you're able to teach your children how they should be, not just when you're "mom-ing" them. You're constantly modeling what they should do in any situation—all of it: the good, the bad, and the downright hideous. One of my favorite poems is "Children Learn What They Live" by Dorothy Law Nolte, PhD. This poem helped me to understand the kind of mom I want to be based on the type of kids I want to have. I've also been able to better understand other people by imagining what they may have lived.

If children live with criticism, they learn to condemn.

If children live with hostility, they learn to fight.

If children live with fear, they learn to be apprehensive.

If children live with pity, they learn to feel sorry for themselves.

If children live with ridicule, they learn to feel shy.

If children live with jealousy, they learn to feel envy.

If children live with shame, they learn to feel guilty.

If children live with encouragement, they learn confidence.

If children live with tolerance, they learn patience.

If children live with praise, they learn appreciation.

If children live with acceptance, they learn to love.

If children live with approval, they learn to like themselves.

If children live with recognition, they learn it is good to have a goal.

If children live with sharing, they learn generosity.

If children live with honesty, they learn truthfulness.

If children live with fairness, they learn justice.

If children live with kindness and consideration, they learn respect.

If children live with security, they learn to have faith in themselves and in those about them.

If children live with friendliness, they learn the world is a nice place in which to live.

Being Our Best Selves Does NOT = Perfection

All of us want to be people who only demonstrate the positives. We want to be the best possible parents. We know that our children deserve the best of us, and we want to give that to them. We want our sons and daughters to be better than we were and do more than we did. That's our natural instinct and how our species continues to evolve. But we all know there are things in life that happen that interfere with us being "perfect" or sometimes even semiperfect parents. Life can throw some real badass curveballs, and with that, we revert to survival mode. We don't always have the luxury of being our best selves. Bottom line is that no one is perfect. The "perfect mom" we all want to be doesn't exist anywhere, and neither does the "perfect dad" or "perfect spouse." Everyone has their thing(s) that they work on and deal with. The most important thing to remember is that your family doesn't need a perfect version of you; they need a striving version of you. They need a person who accepts her faults and marvels at her strengths, but more than anything, they need a mom who does her very best to be a peaceful and happy person. Achieving this balance and example will be the greatest accomplishment of your life. It's one of those things that seems very simple but that in practice can be very difficult.

My husband and I took our two rambunctious boys to a friend's son's birthday party. It was a warm summer afternoon with a beautiful blue sky. The kids were enjoying the pool party, and there was a wonderful spread of goodies, like big sugar cookies, chips, pretzels, a veggie tray, hamburgers, and hot dogs, and, to wash it all down, there were water bottles and a variety of soft drinks. In true Brazilian fashion, my husband and I let our boys select what they wanted at the party because, well, it *was* a party. We had an idea of what they were getting but weren't monitoring every single crumb to cross their lips. We were keeping an eye on them like good, responsible parents but letting them have a lot of autonomy even for their younger ages. Unsurprisingly to me, they didn't make a beeline for the veggies, and that was fine. We were there to party, after all.

In contrast, the majority of the other parents had strict rules for their kids, like that they were allowed to have only a certain number of pretzels and absolutely no soda or chips, but more veggies, and that the kids had to split a sugar cookie with a sibling. Absolutely no judgment here, as I really admire these ladies. I also believe that parents know what's best for their own children. I'm in no way a nutritionist, nor do I claim to have the answers to parenting. However, I did notice that a few of the moms were becoming stressed by the level of surveillance needed to monitor their children's food choices. One of them copped an attitude with her son for picking the sugar cookie over the veggies. Many of the other families ran into the same situations, and, as a result, their stress levels increased due to being in this non-diet-friendly environment.

One of the dads came over to my husband and me and expressed his amazement at how our sons were given free rein yet didn't seem to overindulge and seemed calmer than the other kids who had more restrictions. How could it be that our boys were consuming more sugar than the others but were calmer? The dad said, "I mean, with the amount of soda your son has consumed [one paper party cup], I would think he would be bouncing off the walls, but he's not! And here we are, stressing out about the half of a cookie we'll give our daughter, and she's going nuts. I noticed this at the other parties we've been to together and just want to tell you that I like your approach. No one is getting stressed, everyone is having a good time in your family, and the kids are relatively calm." We explained that we make exceptions for parties and let the kids enjoy the goodies guilt-free. They can relax more, and so can we. We also explained some of the cultural differences with my husband being Brazilian. The other father loved the idea.

The cool part about this whole thing is that the other parent noticed the dynamic of our family compared to some of the other families and saw that it was calmer and easier, in a way. It wasn't a conversation about nutrition but actually about approach. Do we give our kids free rein all day, every day? No, of course not! We encourage them to make healthy choices but also discuss how to enjoy themselves with occasional treats at a party.

In my perspective, the parents who were closely monitoring everything their child tried to consume didn't enjoy themselves as much as they could have with a lighter perspective. I'm all for rules and systems and teaching kids the right choices they should be making. I respect that these are all very personal decisions. I believe that more conversations need to take place prior to getting to that party than at the actual party, which sometimes turns out to be a conversation in a frustrated, elevated tone in front of others. Like I said before, there are no perfect parents. I'm not a perfect mom by any stretch of the imagination. I have family members who gasp in horror to see our kids drinking soda occasionally. I have been that mom to talk to my kids in an elevated, frustrated tone in front of others. In this example, though, my biggest point is that in striving for perfection (controlling what their children ate to an extreme), there was a sacrifice being made, which was the enjoyment of the party. A couple of the kids moped around after being scolded for eating a sugar cookie, and a couple of the moms were just beside themselves. No perfect parents exist. If you're looking for perfection, please realize that something else will always have to give in order for that one area to have the illusion of perfection.

Think again about the words of the poem by Dr. Nolte and consider, in the quest of perfection, what were the parents teaching their children indirectly? If you aren't sure what you may be teaching your children without realizing it, think about what makes you lose your cool with your kids. What are your triggers? What are your tough situations? How do you react in those moments? What does that indirectly teach your kids? Does that line up with what you want to teach them? What would be a better approach to use in those situations?

A Woman of Many Hats

Your roles as a mom and wife are the biggest and most important parts of your life. However, you're a woman of many hats. You're a daughter and maybe a sister, aunt, cousin, friend, coworker, gym buddy, neighbor, community member, and many more. Each of these areas is important and worthy of our time. We need to be open to exploring each of these roles and evaluating them. How can we be a better daughter? How can we be a better friend? Do we need to step up the amount of time and energy we are putting into any of our relationships? Do we need to reduce some of the time we are investing in some relationships? Are there any relationships we need to cut out completely? Is there a role you've either willingly or unwillingly taken on that isn't a good match for your current season of life? Take inventory of where your time and energy are going. How would you like your life to be in these areas, and what needs to change to get you closer to that desire?

Remember that nothing has to change overnight, but small changes over time add up to major life shifts. If you persistently follow your best choice according to your current phase of life, you'll always be on the best path to where you want to go. It's our day-to-day choices and disciplines that will determine our overall greatness. Planning can become your best friend to help you off the ground. You can either make a checklist of what you'd like to do weekly and refer to it throughout the week to keep you on track, or you could plan out the whole month or more ahead of time and stick to it.

If this all feels like too much to juggle and do, I totally get it. It's a whole lot! But I do believe it's possible to have it all. However, I know from experience that it's not realistic to expect to have it all every single day. Striving for perfection in any of these areas will cause the other areas to suffer. I also believe in giving your absolute best, but I would like to differentiate between giving your best and achieving perfection. There are so many areas of parenting that are totally, 100 percent out of your control. Hell, even if you aren't a parent, there are millions of things out of your control. But what I'm saying is that in giving your best, you can feel good about the effort you're putting forth. You can be proud of the progress, however small, you're making. If your goal is to be perfect or have any of the above categories be perfect, you're not only chasing a mirage, but you're choosing to sacrifice some of the best parts of your life.

If you're striving for the perfect career, you'll need to sacrifice other areas sometimes. If you're focusing on the lack of that perfect career, the more it will elude you, and the more you'll miss out on present happiness. You won't be able to enjoy the party. Imperfections are inevitable, but they're also incredible. It's in those moments of realizing imperfections that we become aware of the necessary growth. In that awareness, a seed of desire is planted. We're setting up a new trajectory for ourselves. If we resist that and complain about those moments, the process takes much longer. We can't easily propel ourselves forward. We get stuck in that discontented moment that we know is not a place of love and growth.

Mom Guilt is a Real Bitch

When we are wearing our many hats and doing all of the things that make us who we are, it's easy to get hung up on the wrong ideas about what's missing—cue the mom guilt. Yes, we immensely love and adore our children, and we also realize this motherhood thing can be incredibly difficult at times. It's because of this immense love that we don't want to eff it up, and we feel *reallllllly* guilty when we do. Mom guilt is a common thread for all moms across the board. We've all been there and will probably be there again next week. There's a whole YouTube series that I've created on mom guilt and how to ditch it for good. http://www.embracethebeautifulchaos.com/media

A common motive for this guilt is that we would love to do something for ourselves but feel bad because (we believe) we should be doing something for our kids. It's almost like we forget that we have needs, too. I hear all the time, "I would love to _____, but it's hard with the kids." Or "I know I should _____, but I just feel bad taking that time for myself. What if the kids need me?" Mom guilt is heavy and suffocating. You need to question your guilt and get to the underlying root of it. For example, if you fall into the "I would love to do a Zumba class once a week, but I feel bad taking that time for myself" category, don't be discouraged! Question it.

Here's what questioning might look like:

Why do I feel bad about taking one to two hours out of my day for myself?

I mean, after all, it's for a good cause. I'll be exercising and having fun. I can be a better version of myself if I have time away from the kids and daily demands. The healthier I am, the more energy I'll have. I'll be setting a good example for my kids. I do feel a little lazy, though, about having to get everything ready for me to leave. I mean, the class is only at 7 p.m., and it's a little easier just to stay home and push through the mayhem than to plan things out and get myself there.

It's so much work to get everything ready for someone to watch the kids while I go to this class.

Is it really *a lot* work? What are the things I'd need to do in order to go? I could bump shower time up earlier that one night and have everyone fed by the time the sitter arrives (or by the time I need to leave), or I could write a quick list for my spouse for things to do with the kids while I'm away. I guess it wouldn't be too hard. I could make this a quick-and-easy dinner night, which would help as well. I like that the class is on a night when we don't have any other commitments.

If any other resistance or reasons why this won't work surface in this area, create the next question around that resistance topic.

What's the worst that could happen?

The worst that could happen is that one or more of my kids would cry for the entire time I'm away. They may be so upset that they don't eat anything. They will be mad at me for leaving. I will feel bad and not enjoy the class. OK, now what's the probability of this really happening? Not very likely that any of this will happen. I will only know for sure by trying it out.

What's the best that could happen?

This will become something I look forward to every week, and the kids will as well. If a babysitter comes, that's amazing, because she will have fresh energy and ideas to engage and play with the kids. If my spouse is home, it'll be a great chance for him and the kids to bond. The dynamic always changes when people leave, often in a positive way. This can become a fun night for the kids. It'll be a chance for my husband to see the shenanigans I get a first-row seat for each day and bring him to a greater appreciation of our family and of me. I'll get in better shape. I'll be happy. I can swing by Target afterward and wander the aisles while sipping my Starbucks and just enjoy myself. This will be amazing! I'm looking forward to this time.

Who will watch the kids? (This might be a loaded question for either financial or other reasons, but go deeper into this.)

Maybe this question triggers worry about money. If that's the case, you can always offer to swap babysitting with another mom or find another cost-effective alternative. I understand how a simple activity can add up quickly if you're paying for someone to watch your kids. You have the babysitter cost, the cost of the meal while you are away (I usually feel the need to buy pizza or something for this type of event), plus the cost of the activity you're going to for yourself. Add in gas money and a possible on-demand movie, and you're way over the original cost of a Zumba class. But there are always ways to get creative and save money. It doesn't have to be a spend fest just because mama is away for a bit.

Maybe your reluctance isn't about money as much as it is about having to ask someone for a favor. I've been known to have a difficult time asking for help from others. I would rather just do it myself. This can even go for asking my husband for something like this, but it also extends to asking other family and friends for favors. Well, let me tell you that if you don't ask, they'll never know that you even want to do a Zumba class or whatever. They won't know that you need time for yourself so you don't lose your shit. They won't just magically offer to watch your kids on that day and time. It's OK to speak up and voice your desires. It's actually more than OK; it's necessary. Once I got this, my life changed for the better. I realized I was getting pretty good at anticipating others' needs. I instinctively know when my kids are getting hungry or that my husband would like a massage. I don't always proactively offer these, but I have trained myself to become acutely aware of their needs. Unfortunately, this tends to be mostly a mom thing to do. However, let's not sit around and pout about this reality but understand that people are willing and happy to help us if they know we would like help. Let's find our voices and speak up. You already have the "no" as long as you don't ask, so ask to increase your chances of getting that "yes."

158 All the Jobs Moms Do

If emotions come up regarding asking certain people, you can question that too. If your sister will watch the kids but usually gives you a hard time about doing it, question why that happens or why it bothers you. Dive deep into each area of uneasiness, and in that place, you will usually find your solution.

Do I believe that I deserve this time?

Do I feel bad about taking this time because I don't think I have the right to do so? Did my mom take time for herself? Am I worried that my kids will think I don't love them if I do things for myself when I could be with them? What's the bigger picture here—will an hour or two really make a difference for my kids in the long term? If I were with them, would I be positively engaging with them, or would they be playing on their own while I'm doing my own thing anyway? Go as deeply as you can on this topic, you will uncover a lot of info here that may have been hidden in plain sight.

Whatever comes up for you, it's OK to honor where you are and question your perception, expectations, and beliefs. It's safe to ask yourself questions to better understand what your real issue is. If we are willing to take a closer look, we will always find the root. Once we find the root, we can begin to heal and to rewrite our beliefs. There's guilt-free relief on the other side of our questions. We can be the mom that we want to be through introspection and willingness to grow. It's good to feel good. We owe it to ourselves, our families, and everyone we come in contact with.

My Wish for You

There is a Japanese worldview called wabi-sabi, in which the focus is on acceptance of the imperfection and transience of life. It's finding beauty in the imperfect, impermanent, and incomplete. A lot of times we overlook what's right in front of our noses because we're searching for perfection and the fantasy world we create in our minds of how our lives and families *should* look, act, and be, and then we're disappointed when our reality doesn't mirror that perfection. My wish for you is that you take the wabi-sabi approach in your lives, finding joy and beauty in the imperfections. Wabi-sabi encourages you to find the fascinating and beautiful in the most basic and often overlooked things and phases of life. This approach creates appreciation for the imperfect and ever-changing parts of motherhood as we realize each season will not last forever.

The first major wabi-sabi breakthrough I had was to willingly purchase my minivan. I remember being dead set against a minivan in my life for a couple of decades. I was *not* going to be *that person* (whatever that was supposed to mean). I had considered spending close to $100,000 that I didn't have to avoid getting the minivan. I had an idea in my mind that minivans weren't cool, and I had to have an SUV because they were better and better for me. The thought of pulling up to the curb in a minivan was beyond embarrassing to me. I vowed that I would never buy one, no matter what!

Well, life has a funny way of working, and I was pregnant with my daughter (our third child) when I needed a new car. My family often has relatives and friends visiting, and we needed extra seating in our car. A lot of SUVs only have seven seats, with the backseats being cramped, which isn't a good idea for my tall family. I wanted something luxurious. I wanted something that I would feel good in. I wanted something that worked for my family and me. After many coincidental encounters and being surprised by many unprompted conversations of people raving about their minivans—how amazing they are for their kids and how much better their lives were by having a minivan—I was slightly intrigued. A definite tipping point was when one of my neighbors had "upgraded" her vehicle from a minivan to a luxury SUV. We asked her about the newer SUV since that's what we were looking into, and her comment floored me. She said, "I honestly miss the van. Would pick that over this any day."

Say whaaaat?? That was a moment when my perception significantly shifted regarding minivans. My neighbor went on to point out her favorite aspects of her minivan, which happened to be all the things we were looking for. She was describing our wish list for our next car. Cue the wabi-sabi shift—I realized that my kids would only be kids for a phase. That phase wouldn't last forever and would most likely coincide with how long we would keep the new car. As I embraced the wabi-sabi part of the situation, I noticed that I wasn't giving up anything permanently and that I would only have this car for a certain period in my life. I could see the beauty in the features this particular vehicle would offer to my family for this phase. Talk about doing a 180! A year or two after getting the minivan, we purchased a luxury SUV for my husband when his car died, and I'm the first to say that I prefer the van. I just smile when I say things like that because of how adamant I was about never, ever wanting one, but it has been a fantastic choice for me and the fam. It's now already five years old!

My wish for you is that you see the wabi-sabi in each phase of your life. There will be a lot of imperfections but also a lot of beauty. I wish you an easy time recognizing the beauty and goodness of this phase of life and that you know with all certainty that you will see it if you're looking for it. If your focus is on what's missing and what you wish it were like instead, you're turning a blind eye to all of the beauty available to you now. So I wish that you will always remain open to the glimmers of joy and beauty in the midst of the chaos and messiness of your life. I wish you days filled with warm hugs, sweet kisses, and time well spent with your loved ones. I wish you time to invest in yourself for your sanity and well-being. I wish you peace during the grocery store meltdowns and the exhausting bedtime routines. I wish you the sight to view the best in your children, your spouse, and yourself, today and always.

#embracethebeautifulchaos

OK, fine, but how do I apply this IRL?

You know what you want to teach your children and understand the best way to do that is often through your example. You know perfection doesn't exist, and you're committed to seeing the beauty in the many imperfections of motherhood. You've figured out that the best way to change your life is by changing yourself. Taking time to reflect on questions from this chapter will provide you with a deeper understanding of yourself and how you live your life, indirectly teaching your children how to live theirs. Let the mom guilt guide you to a deeper understanding of yourself by asking those important questions and exploring it. If you continue to ask the tough questions of yourself and explore your emotions as they come up, taking time to reenergize and refresh yourself, you will thrive as you embrace your beautiful chaos. You know that some days will be easier than others, and that's Ok. But no matter what is happening in your world, you will be at peace.

Embrace the Magic of Affirmations

* I choose to have fun with my kids.
* I choose to enjoy my family.
* I am doing my best every day.
* My children are my best teachers.
* I handle every situation with love and understanding.

PART 4

Troubleshooting:
Help a Mama Out!

Troubleshooting: Help a Mama Out!

OK, so you are all nice and Zen AF, but then something happens, and you feel like you're going to lose your shit! Help a mom out!! Check out this quick list of ideas to try in the heat of the moment to stay sane in the beautiful chaos of your life.

Breathe

Have you noticed that breathing and anger don't really go well together? You just flip and explode. No pause, no space, no chance. The next time you notice that you begin to feel overwhelmed, frustrated, or like you will lose it, take a breath in for a count of five, hold that breath for a count of five, then release the breath for a count of five. Repeat this at least three times. Notice that you now feel calmer and can better handle whatever was throwing you off. The magic of counting on the inhale, hold, and exhale helps us to calm the hell down and not lose our shit because it provides that buffer that we need to recenter.

Set Your Intentions

Set the intention to respond, not react. Take a minute if you need it to gain composure and then return to the situation, ready to respond like the mom you'd like to be instead of reacting, or worse, overreacting, and regretting it later. This intention setting moment could be a little self pep-talk or reminder. Imagine someone you admire as a mom is unbiasedly observing you in that crazy moment. What advice would they give to you? That can be your intention.

Affirmations

How you talk to yourself matters, especially in tough moments. Have an affirmation or two up your sleeve for situations that threaten your peace. These go-to mantras can be used at any time and can change over time. It's important to find phrases that resonate with what helps you feel better at that moment. If you're looking for some inspiration, check out my card deck filled with magical affirmations especially for moms. For more info, check my website at www.embracethebeautifulchaos.com/resources

Sing

When the kids have me at my wits' end, the song that usually comes to mind first is DMX's "Y'all Gonna Make Me Lose My Mind," and I'll sing that aloud. Another one I like to whip out, usually during a fit, is the Fugees's "Killing Me Softly." The options here are endless. When there's something that the kids really, really want in the store but I say no and then they whine and start to revolt, I summon my inner Jagger and serenade them with Rolling Stones's "You Can't Always Get What You Want." I could go on and on, but the song doesn't have to be an actual correlation to the situation. You can sing any song you like to feel better at that moment. Let the music be your much-needed release in that moment.

Humor

Try to find the existing humor in a tough situation or pull in humor somehow. There are days that this is easier for me than others, but I've come to learn that my children voicing their opposing opinions isn't automatically an attack on me as a mom. Usually, they just don't want to go to bed. It tends to go much better for everyone if we keep humor involved. This can mean talking in a silly voice, making an appropriate joke, or remembering a recent funny time that you shared together.

Pray

After your deep breath, say a little prayer, whatever that may look or sound like for you, asking for guidance to resolve your problem and help to see your situation with love. Listen to the voice or thought that first comes and be ready for major shifts! Your prayer doesn't have to be formal or anything fancy, either. A little authentic prayer goes a long way, especially for moms.

Change of Scenery

If possible, get out and breathe some fresh air. Look up at the sky. Go for a walk in nature, specifically by some water. If you can't do that, pull up the sound of rain, the ocean, a river, or a waterfall on the Internet and close your eyes for a few moments, imagining you're in that beautiful place. This is usually a quick reset for me. There's something so calming about being in nature.

Observe

Just be a quiet observer in the moment. Notice what you're seeing on the outside as well as what's going on inside your body. Notice what emotions are coming up and how they lessen when you simply observe.

Question It

How are your expectations in this moment? How are your emotions? What can you learn in this moment? What is truly in your control? How can you choose to think, act, and be?

Go Easy

If you ended up losing your shit, go easy on yourself! If you snapped, yelled, or reacted in a way you wish you wouldn't have, be gentle with yourself. Take time to reflect on the situation and discuss it with your child (or whoever you flipped out on) when calm. Ask for forgiveness when needed and use the teachable moment to model what to do when you mess up. We're all human, after all.

Bigger Perspective

Remind yourself that this was one event of the day. In no way, shape, or form does it need to alter the remainder of the day. You can let it go and move on with grace and ease. Yes, it was annoying, but it's not worth ruining any more of your precious time over.

Talk It Over

Talk about it with your spouse, relative, or friend. Sometimes another set of eyes can see what we cannot. Be sure to only contact people who will lift you higher, not someone who will drag you down and keep you in the negativity of the moment. It's fine to feel angry about something that happened. Share that with someone, but only to process it and move past the anger and into understanding.

Tap on It: EFT—Emotional Freedom Technique

This is also known as tapping, which is a technique to quickly gain a significant reduction of stress, overwhelm, fear, etc. by tapping on set meridian points on the body. There are many guided tapping sessions on YouTube that are specifically designed for whatever you're feeling at that moment. EFT is most helpful to me when I'm really worked up about something and need relief. I want to feel better, but I'm just too anxious or too angry, and that's when I know I need to tap on whatever is bothering me. To find the best match for what I'm going through, I search "EFT for anxiety," "EFT for anger," or "EFT for overwhelm" and follow the guided sessions.

Meditation

So many types to choose from! I'm not always in a frame of mind where I can meditate "traditionally"—you know, the whole sitting crisscross applesauce on an embroidered pillow with my eyes closed in silence, clear minded for twenty minutes or something, even though that sounds pretty cool. So, an amazing resource for me has been guided meditations. There are so many free ones on YouTube with varying lengths and focuses. My favorite guided meditation that I use with all of my clients is available for free on my website at http://www.embracethebeautifulchaos.com/resources

There are also kundalini meditations, which have been helpful to me as well. One of my faves for when motherhood is especially tough is called the Kirtan Kriya. The words that are chanted are "sa, ta, na, ma," and they mean "peace begins with me." As the words are being spoken or sung, you move your fingers into different mudras. There are four mudras that accompany the four words:

1. Say "peace" or "sa" as you press your index finger and thumb together (I like to use both hands).
2. Say "begins" or "ta" as you press your middle finger and thumb together.
3. Say "with" or "na" as you press your ring finger and thumb together.
4. Say "me" or "ma" as you press your pinky and thumb together.

Repeat this sequence for three to twelve minutes.

There is a wonderful guided version of the Kirtan Kriya on YouTube, of course. Like anything in life, the most important thing is to find what works for you that day and what makes you feel balanced.

Energy Work

Look into energy healing. Many practitioners can do remote sessions so that you can benefit from treatment in the comfort of your own home. I worked with my therapist from a suburb of Philadelphia while she was in Sao Paulo, Brazil. A special shoutout to Simone Gentile at Energia Quantica for teaching and mentoring me over the years.

There is info on my website if you'd like to work with me on your energy healing. https://embracethebeautifulchaos.com/coaching

You Are Ready to Embrace Your Beautiful Chaos

You've probably noticed by now that your day-to-day "chaos" hasn't changed much in terms of quantity since you started this book. I bet it's safe to say that you still experience that whirlwind on the daily, right? But what has changed by now, my dear, is *you*. Give yourself a huge hug or a pat on the back for making it through this book. I've asked you to do some pretty big things in these pages, and here you are, living proof of a more peaceful and happier woman, automatically making you a better mom.

Celebrate your success! I'm proud of you and honor your growth so far on this journey! Revisit this book any time you need a reminder of how marvelous you are, Mama. Keep up the wonderful work, and continue to make yourself a priority, you glorious badass goddess! The tools and habits you've created will take you forward on your journey of staying true to yourself amid the beautiful chaos.

Better Together

You now have the awareness and tools to happily embrace your beautiful chaos. Once again, I'm so proud of you and all of the work you have done so far! I'd be lying if I told you that your work is complete, though. You'll still need to go within yourself to find your balance and peace as we talked about in this book, but there's something extremely powerful and uplifting about joining together with other women who are in the same motherhood boat as you. So, come and join me and other moms who are on this journey to fully embrace as much of the beautiful chaos as we can. You'll find ongoing support and solutions as you continue along your journey.

www.embracethebeautifulchaos.com

iamstephaniepereira

Stephanie Pereira @embracethebeautifulchaos

Embrace the Beautiful Chaos

Embrace the Beautiful Chaos

#embracethebeautifulchaos

Notes

Coop & Casey, "62% of Philadelphians Who Want to Get in Shape Say This Is the #1 Reason They Haven't Gone to the Gym Yet," 96.5TDY, accessed February 19, 2020, https://965tdy.radio.com/blogs/coop-casey/coop-casey-62-philadelphians-who-want-get-shape-say-1-reason-they-havent-gone-gym.

Yes Man, directed by Peyton Reed (Burbank: Warner Bros, 2008), DVD.

Bad Moms, directed by Jon Lucas and Scott Moore (Burbank: STX Entertainment, 2016) DVD.

Rebecca Dube, "Moms Confess: Husband versus Kids, Who Stresses Them Out More?" Today, May 11, 2013, https://www.today.com/parents/moms-confess-husband-versus-kids-who-stresses-them-out-more-1C9884930.

Thomas Gordon, PhD, "Origins of the Gordon Model," Gordon Training International, accessed February 19, 2020, https://www.gordontraining.com/thomas-gordon/origins-of-the-gordon-model/.

Brittany Gibbons, "My Husband and I Had Sex Every Day for a Year— Here's How We are Doing Now," *Good Housekeeping*, August 29, 2016.

Elisabeth Lloyd, *The Case of the Female Orgasm: Bias in the Science of Evolution* (Cambridge, MA: The Harvard Press, 2006), 63–64.

Jordan Page (*FunCheaporFree*), "The 'Block Schedule' System—Life changing Productivity Hack!" YouTube, August 30, 2018, https://www.youtube.com/watch?v=2BKuSlstIBM.

Rachel Harris and Dorothy Law Nolte, *Children Learn What They Live* (New York: Workman Publishing Co. Inc., 1998), 82–84.

About the Author

STEPHANIE PEREIRA is a mom of 3 who has discovered tangible ways to improve her day-to-day perspective on motherhood, marriage and her life. In her book, *Embrace the Beautiful Chaos of Motherhood*, blog, coaching and workshops, she shares relatable real-life examples so her audience can find their Zen as well.

Stephanie has worked in a variety of fields, from selling airplanes to teaching 8th grade math to being an at-home mom. Every stage of that journey has brought her to this point where she helps other moms navigate through motherhood with more peace, ease and enjoyment. She lives with her family in the Philadelphia area and enjoys dancing with her husband, reading to her kids, training Muay Thai and traveling with her family.

Stephanie's no stranger to being an exhausted, stressed-out mom. Her long-time anxiety and occasional panic attacks were a result of giving her full attention and focus to her family while totally overlooking her self-care (mental, emotional, spiritual, physical.) She knows firsthand how easily consumed moms can become and how quickly they can become overwhelmed. That leads to actions and reactions that bring on mom guilt, which leads to more overwhelm and to more undesired actions and reactions. After several years of consistent self-care on all fronts accompanied by learning lots of strategies to handle mom overwhelm, the peace Stephanie feels the majority of the time is something that she wishes for all moms.

She has seen how easy it is for herself and for her mom friends to fall off the peace wagon. So, she wrote this book describing the lessons and tips she's learned over the years for others to use as well. She hopes that frazzled moms will explore these strategies and perspectives, take what works best for them, and spark a personal journey which will continue well beyond this book. To learn more or contact Stephanie, visit www.embracethebeautifulchaos.com.